Take a Hike!

An Exercise Book for Mt. Κοίνη

GREEK FOR EVERYONE

Copyright © 2017 by Maury Robertson.

All rights reserved. No part of this publication may be reproduced, distributed or transmitted in any form or by any means, including photocopying, recording, or other electronic or mechanical methods, without the prior written permission of the publisher, except in the case of brief quotations embodied in critical reviews and certain other noncommercial uses permitted by copyright law. For permission requests, write to the publisher, addressed "Attention: Permissions Coordinator," at the address below.

Maury Robertson/Anchorpoint Press
2443 Fillmore St. 380 2427
San Francisco, CA 94115

http://greekforeveryone.com

Take a Hike/ Maury Robertson. —1st ed.

ISBN-10: 0-9994916-1-X
ISBN-13: 978-0-9994916-1-4

Πάτερ ἡμῶν
ὁ ἐν τοῖς οὐρανοῖς,

ἁγιασθήτω τὸ ὄνομά σου·
ἐλθέτω ἡ βασιλεία σου·
γενηθήτω τὸ θέλημά σου,

ὡς ἐν οὐρανῷ, καὶ ἐπὶ γῆς·

τὸν ἄρτον ἡμῶν τὸν ἐπιούσιον δὸς ἡμῖν σήμερον·

καὶ ἄφες ἡμῖν τὰ ὀφειλήματα ἡμῶν,
ὡς καὶ ἡμεῖς ἀφίεμεν τοῖς ὀφειλέταις ἡμῶν·

καὶ μὴ εἰσενέγκῃς ἡμᾶς εἰς πειρασμόν,
ἀλλὰ ῥῦσαι ἡμᾶς ἀπὸ τοῦ πονηροῦ.

Ὅτι σοῦ ἐστιν ἡ βασιλεία
καὶ ἡ δύναμις
καὶ ἡ δόξα
εἰς τοὺς αἰῶνας.

Ἀμήν.

Base Camp — 1
1. Grammar Overview — 2
2. The Greek Alphabet — 4
3. Vowels, Diphthongs, Syllables, Punctuation — 9
4. Pronunciation, Accents, Breathing Marks — 13

The Crossroads — 17
5. Conjunctions — 18
6. Prepositions — 20

Noun Rest — 25
7. Nouns — 26
8. First Declension — 27
9. Second Declension — 31
10. Third Declension — 35

Camp Modifier — 39
11. The Article — 40
12. 2-1-2 Adjectives — 43
13. 3-1-3 Adjectives — 45
14. 2-2 & 3-3 Adjectives — 48
15. Adjective Usage — 53

Pronoun Point — 55
16. First & Second Person Pronouns — 56
17. Third Person Pronouns — 60
18. Relative Pronouns — 64
19. Interrogative and Indefinite Pronouns — 67
20. Demonstrative and Reflexive Pronouns — 70

Valley of the Verbs — 75
21. Tense, Voice, Mood, Person, Number — 76
22. Personal Endings — 78
23. Contract Verbs — 80
24. Regular Roots and Stems — 81
25. Adverbs — 82

The Labyrinth — 83
- 26. Liquid Verbs — 84
- 27. Second Aorists — 87
- 28. Deponents — 90
- 29. Principal Parts — 94
- 30. μι verbs, εἰμί — 96

Moody Outlook — 99
- 31. Subjunctive Mood — 100
- 32. Imperative Mood — 103
- 33. Infinitives — 106

Participle Panorama — 109
- 34. Participles Overview — 110
- 35. Present Participles — 112
- 36. Aorist Participles — 115
- 37. Perfect Participles — 118

ANSWERS

Base Camp — 123
- 1. Grammar Overview — 124
- 3. Vowels, Diphthongs, Syllables, Punctuation — 125
- 4. Pronunciation, Accents, Breathing Marks — 126

The Crossroads — 129
- 5. Conjunctions — 130
- 6. Prepositions — 131

Noun Rest — 133
- 7. Nouns — 134
- 8. First Declension — 135
- 9. Second Declension — 136
- 10. Third Declension — 137

Camp Modifier — 139
- 11. The Article — 140

12. 2-1-2 Adjectives	141
13. 3-1-3 Adjectives	142
14. 2-2 & 3-3 Adjectives	144
15. Adjective Usage	146

Pronoun Point — 147

16. First and Second Person Pronouns	148
17. Third Person Pronouns	151
18. Relative Pronouns	154
19. Interrogative and Indefinite Pronouns	155
20. Demonstrative and Reflexive Pronouns	156

Valley of the Verbs — 159

21. Tense, Voice, Mood, Person, Number	160
22. Personal Endings	162
23. Contract Verbs	164
24. Regular Roots & Stems	165
25. Adverbs	166

The Labyrinth — 167

26. Liquid Verbs	168
27. Second Aorists	170
28. Deponents	172
29. Principal Parts	174
30. μι verbs, εἰμί	175

Moody Outlook — 177

31. Subjunctive Mood	178
32. Imperative Mood	180
33. Infinitives	182

Participle Panorama — 185

34. Participles Overview	186
35. Present Participles	188
36. Aorist Participles	192
37. Perfect Participles	195

Base Camp

Know your ABC's

GREEK
FOR EVERYONE

1. Grammar Overview

See if you can fill out the parts of speech from memory. Be certain that you understand the function of each part of speech. Use the Master Chart to check your work.

Parts of Speech		
Substance	**Motion**	**Relationship**

Check Your Comprehension

In the following paragraph:
- Circle the nouns.
- Underline the articles.
- Put a box around the adjectives.
- Cross out the pronouns.

The biggest obstacle to learning Greek is fear.
It causes weak people to give up.
Valiant students fight through fear until they conquer it!

In the following paragraph:
- Circle the verbs.
- Underline the adverbs.
- Put a box around the participles.
- Cross out the infinitives.

Very few people like to exercise.
Even though activities like running and jogging can be enjoyable,
almost no one does these things happily.

In the following paragraph:
- Circle the conjunctions.
- Underline the prepositions.

Julie (and) I love Northern California (but) the heat sometimes drives us <u>up</u> the wall. We do not plan <u>to</u> move (because) we are comfortable <u>in</u> our house.

2. The Greek Alphabet

Practice writing the letters of the Greek alphabet. Say them out loud as you write them.

Alphabet Practice Sheet

α

β

γ

δ

ε

ζ

η

θ

ι

κ

λ

μ

ν

ξ

ο

π

ρ

σ

ς

τ

υ

φ

χ

ψ

ω

Now see if you can reproduce the letters of the Greek alphabet from memory, using the four section as a guide.

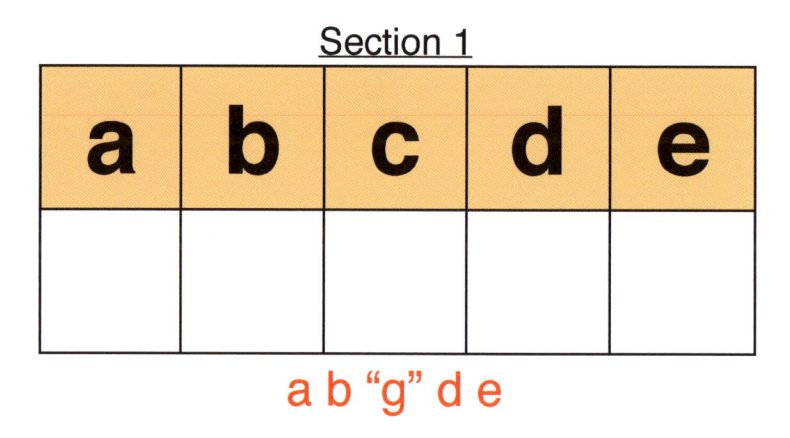

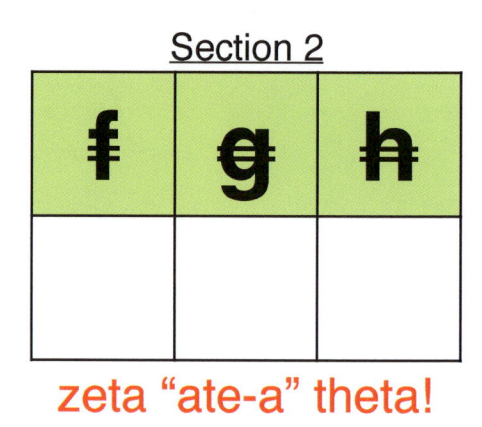

Section 1

a	b	c	d	e

a b "g" d e

Section 2

f	g	h

zeta "ate-a" theta!

Take a Hike! 6

Section 3

i	j	k	l	m	n	( )	o

there is "n o" reason for ξ to be there.
"j" and "q" are junque letters!

Section 3 (continued)

p	q	r	s	t	u

Section 4

v	w	x	y	z

write your own ending
"poughkeepsie, NY"

Take a Hike! 7

Now list the 24 letters of the Greek alphabet from memory.
Do it over and over until it comes easily.

1		13	
2		14	
3		15	
4		16	
5		17	
6		18	
7		19	
8		20	
9		21	
10		22	
11		23	
12		24	

Take a Hike! 8

3. Vowels, Diphthongs, Syllables, Punctuation

1. Write the seven Greek vowels.

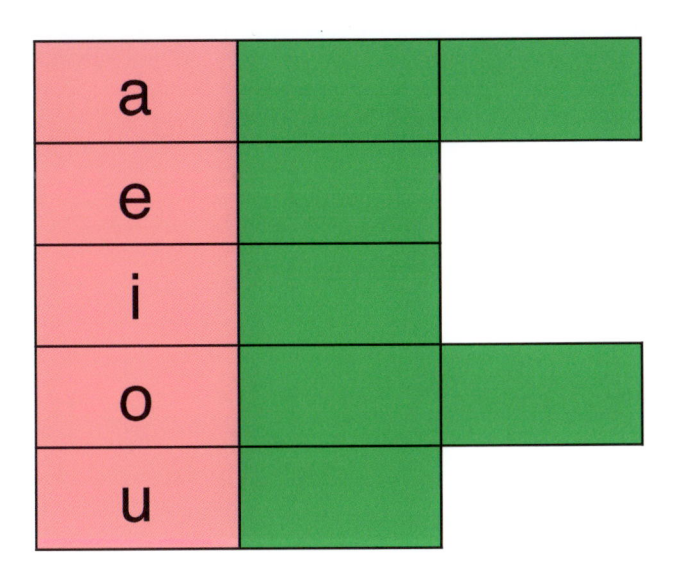

a		
e		
i		
o		
u		

2. What is a diphthong?

3. Write the eight Greek diphthongs.

a	
e	
i	
o	
u	

"we"	
"you"	/

Take a Hike! 9

4. Write the seven Greek vowels again.

5. Write the eight Greek diphthongs again.

6. Underline the vowels or diphthongs in the following words. Next, divide the words into syllables by placing slash marks between them.

   Remember: One syllable per vowel or diphthong.

EXAMPLE

βίβλιον (book)   *becomes*   βί/βλι/ον (book)

κύριος (Lord)	πνεῦμα (Spirit)
μαθητής (disciple)	ἄγγελος (angel)
ἡμέρα (day)	ἁμαρτία (sin)

εἰ (if)	βασιλεία (kingdom)
μετά (with)	δόξα (glory)
οὖν (therefore)	ἔθνος (nation)
πατήρ (father)	ἔργον (deed)
πίστις (faith)	καρδία (heart)
πιστεύω (I believe)	κόσμος (universe)

Supply the English equivalent of the following Greek punctuation.

Greek	English
.	
,	
;	
·	

4. Pronunciation, Accents, Breathing Marks

Draw slash marks between the syllables of John 1:1-5 and practice pronouncing it. (You can check your answers in the back.)

John 1

1 Ἐν ἀρχῇ ἦν ὁ λόγος, καὶ ὁ λόγος ἦν πρὸς τὸν θεόν,
   In (the) beginning was the Word and the Word was with * God

καὶ θεὸς ἦν ὁ λόγος.
and God was the Word.

2 οὗτος ἦν ἐν ἀρχῇ πρὸς τὸν θεόν.
   This one was in (the) beginning with * God.

3 πάντα δι' αὐτοῦ ἐγένετο, καὶ χωρὶς αὐτοῦ ἐγένετο
   Every (thing) through Him (it) came to be and apart from Him (it) came to be

οὐδὲ ἕν.
not even one (thing).

ὃ γέγονεν 4 ἐν αὐτῷ ζωὴ ἦν, καὶ ἡ ζωὴ ἦν τὸ φῶς
That which (it) came to be in Him life was and the life (it) was the light

τῶν ἀνθρώπων·
   * of men.

5 καὶ τὸ φῶς ἐν τῇ σκοτίᾳ φαίνει, καὶ ἡ σκοτία αὐτὸ
   And the light in the darkness (it) is shining and the darkness it

οὐ κατέλαβεν.
not (it) overcame/understood.

Take a Hike! 13

If you want additional practice, work on verses 6-14. The syllabification is given in the answer section, but see if you can figure it out on your own. You may download a slow, medium, and fast pronunciation of John 1 in the resources section.

6 Ἐγένετο ἄνθρωπος, ἀπεσταλμένος παρὰ θεοῦ,
  (he) came   a man   having been sent   from   God

ὄνομα αὐτῷ Ἰωάννης·
  name   to him   John;

7 οὗτος ἦλθεν εἰς μαρτυρίαν ἵνα μαρτυρήσῃ περὶ
  this (man) (he) came unto a witness in order that he might bear witness concerning

τοῦ φωτός, ἵνα πάντες πιστεύσωσιν δι' αὐτοῦ.
  the   light, in order that all (people) (they) might believe through   him.

8 οὐκ ἦν ἐκεῖνος τὸ φῶς, ἀλλ' ἵνα μαρτυρήσῃ περὶ
  Not (he) was that (one) the light but in order that he might bear witness concerning
                                        (he came)

τοῦ φωτός.
  the   light.

9 Ἦν τὸ φῶς τὸ ἀληθινόν, ὃ φωτίζει πάντα
  He was the light the   true   which (it) enlightens every

ἄνθρωπον, ἐρχόμενον εἰς τὸν κόσμον.
  man   coming   into   the   world.

10 ἐν τῷ κόσμῳ ἦν, καὶ ὁ κόσμος δι' αὐτοῦ ἐγένετο,
   In the world He was, and the world through Him (it) came to be

καὶ ὁ κόσμος αὐτὸν οὐκ ἔγνω.
  but the world   Him   not   it knew.

Take a Hike! 14

11 εἰς τὰ ἴδια ἦλθεν, καὶ οἱ ἴδιοι αὐτὸν οὐ
   Into   * His own ones He came and His own ones Him not

παρέλαβον.
they received.

12 ὅσοι δὲ ἔλαβον αὐτόν, ἔδωκεν αὐτοῖς ἐξουσίαν
   As many but (they) received Him   He gave to them authority

τέκνα θεοῦ γενέσθαι, τοῖς πιστεύουσιν εἰς τὸ ὄνομα
children of God to become, to the ones who are believing in the name

αὐτοῦ,
of Him,

13 οἳ οὐκ ἐξ αἱμάτων οὐδὲ ἐκ θελήματος σαρκὸς
   who not from blood and not from (the) will of flesh

οὐδὲ ἐκ θελήματος ἀνδρὸς ἀλλ᾽ ἐκ θεοῦ
and not from (the) will   of a man but from God

ἐγεννήθησαν.
(they) were born.

14 Καὶ ὁ λόγος σὰρξ ἐγένετο καὶ ἐσκήνωσεν ἐν ἡμῖν,
   and the word   flesh (it) came to be and (it) dwelt/tabernacled among us,

καὶ ἐθεασάμεθα τὴν δόξαν αὐτοῦ, δόξαν ὡς
and we beheld the glory of Him/it, glory like

μονογενοῦς παρὰ πατρός, πλήρης χάριτος καὶ
(the) only begotten (one) from (the) Father full of grace and

ἀληθείας.
truth

Take a Hike! 16

The Crossroads
Conjunctions & Prepositions

GREEK
FOR EVERYONE

5. Conjunctions

Underline the conjunctions in the following sentences.

- It is raining tonight but I expect it to stop soon.
- If you keep up this pace then you will soon read Greek like Aristotle did!
- I study Greek in order to develop my vocabulary.
- I am not a fan of country music, nevertheless, I enjoy the concerts.
- Classical musicians do not play the violin like blugrass players do.
- We have been saving money, therefore we will be able go to Europe.
- You will find the keys where I left them under the doormat.
- You will feel spectacular when you master Greek.
- I am hungry and McDonalds has a special on Big Macs so I am going there to eat.
-

Look through John 1 carefully and be sure you are familiar with the conjunctions. These little words will save you a lot of trouble!

Use the interlinear version of John 1 to find the definitions. Write them below each word. You may check your work on the next page.

καί   ἀλλά   οὖν

δέ   ὡς   καθώς

οὐδέ   ὅτι   εἰ

ἵνα   ὅτε   ὅπου

Take a Hike! 18

Conjunctions And Other Little Words You'll See A Lot

ἀλλά	638	but, yet, rather, nevertheless	μή	1042	not (used with non-indicative)
ἄν	166	conditional particle (untrans.)	ὅπου	1042	where
γάρ	1041	for, so, then	ὅταν	123	whenever, when
δέ	2792	but, and, rather, now, then	ὅτε	103	when
ἐάν	351	if, when	ὅτι	1296	that, so that, because, for
εἰ	502	if, that, whether	οὐ	1606	not (used with indicative)
ἕως	146	until, while	οὐδέ	143	and not, neither, nor
ἤ	343	or, either, nor, what, than	οὖν	499	so, therefore, consequently
ἰδού	200	behold, look, see, consider	οὕτως	208	in this manner, thus, so
ἵνα	663	in order that, that, so that	σύν	128	with, together with
καθώς	182	as, just as, even as	τέ	215	and, and so, so
καί	9161	and, even, also, but, yet	τότε	160	then, therefore
μέν	179	on the one hand, indeed	ὡς	504	as, like, because, when, while

6. Prepositions

Underline the prepositions and objects in the following English sentences.

- Over the river and through the woods, to grandmother's house we go!

- There is nowhere I would rather be than sitting beside the lake with a fish on the line.

- I am in love!

- In a year I will be fifty years old.

- Too much partying can get you into trouble.

- I need a get out of jail free card!

- Because of the mortgage meltdown, many American families are under water.

Read over the color coded interlinear translation of John 1. Identify all of the light blue words. (These are prepositions).

Write the meanings for the prepositions you discover in John 1

Greek Word	Meaning
ἐν	
πρός	
διά, δι'	
παρά παρ'	
εἰς	
περί	
ἐκ ἐξ	

Greek Word	Meaning
ὀπίσω	
ἔμπροσθέν	
ἀντί	
πέραν	
ὑπέρ	
ἐπί, επ᾽ εφ	
ἀπό	
πρό	
ὑπό	
ὑποκάτω	

See if you can think of any English words that are formed with Greek prepositions.

Score
12   Genius!
9-11 Not bad!
6-8 Okay
3-5 Think harder
1-2 Come out of your coma!

Greek Word	Meaning	English Cognate(s)
ἐν	in	
διά	through	
πρός	to, toward	
παρά	beside	
εἰς	into	
περί	around	
ἐκ ἐξ	out of	
ἀντι	against	
ὑπέρ	above	
ἐπί	on	
ἀπό	away from	
πρό	before	

Vocabulary

Fill in the prepositions until you can do it from memory. These sixteen prepositions will give you a very good start at recognizing prepositions. There are two more practice diagrams on the next page. Please memorize these prepositions for the quiz. I will supply this diagram and ask you to fill in the Greek prepositions.

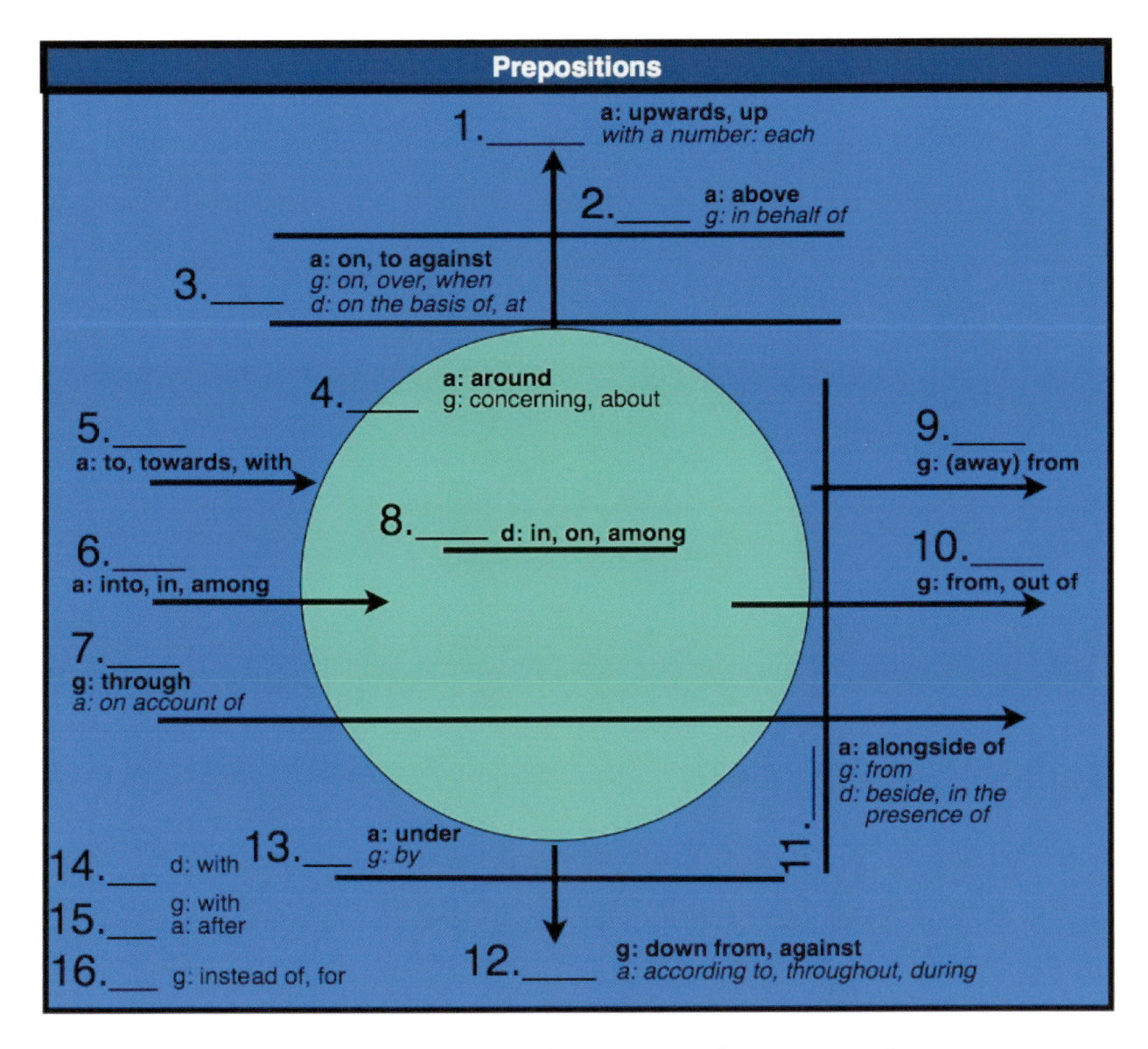

Prepositions

1. ____ a: upwards, up / with a number: each
2. ____ a: above / g: in behalf of
3. ____ a: on, to against / g: on, over, when / d: on the basis of, at
4. ____ a: around / g: concerning, about
5. ____ a: to, towards, with
6. ____ a: into, in, among
7. ____ g: through / a: on account of
8. ____ d: in, on, among
9. ____ g: (away) from
10. ____ g: from, out of
11. ____ a: alongside of / g: from / d: beside, in the presence of
12. ____ g: down from, against / a: according to, throughout, during
13. ____ a: under / g: by
14. ____ d: with
15. ____ g: with / a: after
16. ____ g: instead of, for

I have provided two additional blanks on the next page for more practice.

Take a Hike! 23

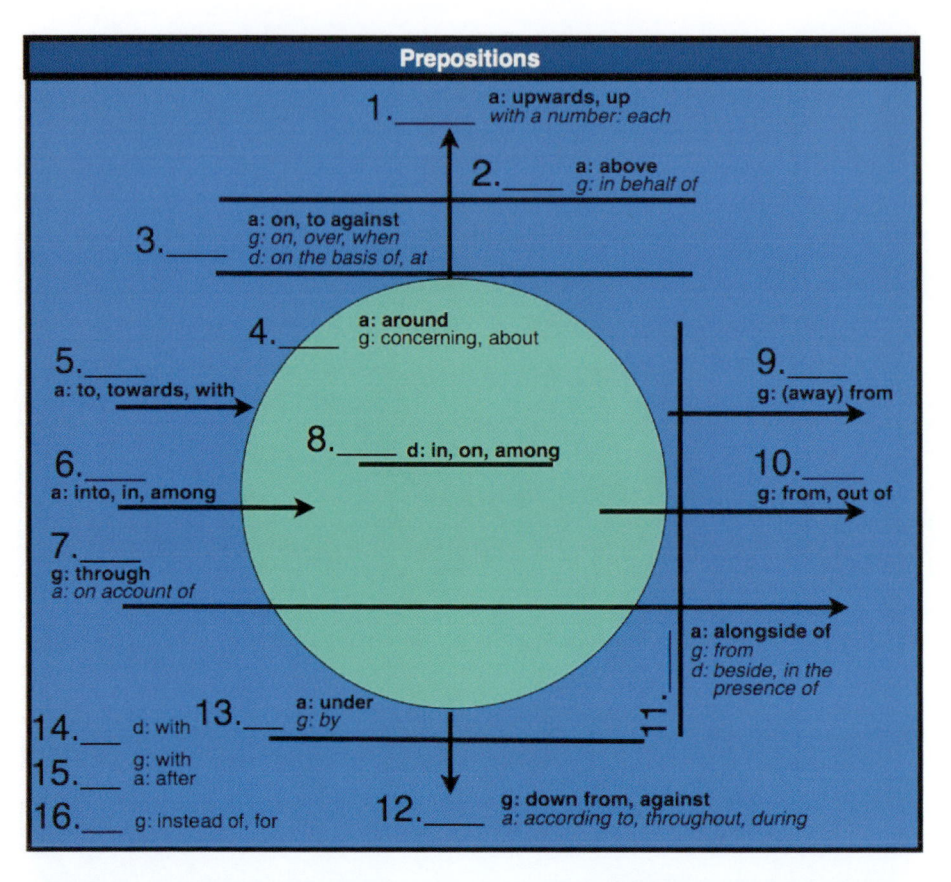

Prepositions

1. _____ a: upwards, up
   with a number: each
2. _____ a: above
   g: in behalf of
3. _____ a: on, to against
   g: on, over, when
   d: on the basis of, at
4. _____ a: around
   g: concerning, about
5. _____ a: to, towards, with
6. _____ a: into, in, among
7. _____ g: through
   a: on account of
8. _____ d: in, on, among
9. _____ g: (away) from
10. _____ g: from, out of
11. _____ a: alongside of
    g: from
    d: beside, in the presence of
12. _____ g: down from, against
    a: according to, throughout, during
13. _____ a: under
    g: by
14. _____ d: with
15. _____ g: with
    a: after
16. _____ g: instead of, for

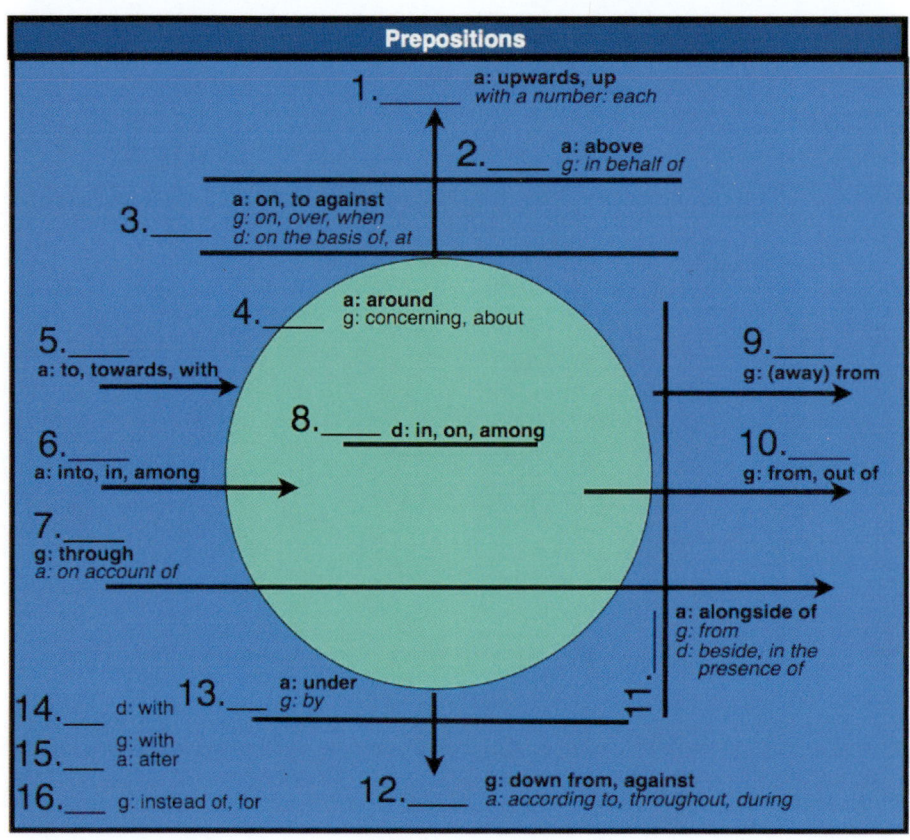

Prepositions

1. _____ a: upwards, up
   with a number: each
2. _____ a: above
   g: in behalf of
3. _____ a: on, to against
   g: on, over, when
   d: on the basis of, at
4. _____ a: around
   g: concerning, about
5. _____ a: to, towards, with
6. _____ a: into, in, among
7. _____ g: through
   a: on account of
8. _____ d: in, on, among
9. _____ g: (away) from
10. _____ g: from, out of
11. _____ a: alongside of
    g: from
    d: beside, in the presence of
12. _____ g: down from, against
    a: according to, throughout, during
13. _____ a: under
    g: by
14. _____ d: with
15. _____ g: with
    a: after
16. _____ g: instead of, for

Take a Hike! 24

Noun Rest

GREEK FOR EVERYONE

7. Nouns

Every Greek noun will be defined by three important attributes:

1. C_____
2. N_____
3. G_____

Fill out the chart below from memory.

Case	Number	Gender
N	S	M
G	P	F
D		N
A		

Match the case with its function in the sentence.

____ Nominative	A	Object of the verb (receives the action)
____ Genitive	B	Indirect object
____ Dative	C	Subject of the verb (does the action)
____ Accusative	D	Possession

True or False

_____ Every Greek noun is either masculine or feminine or neuter.

Take a Hike! 26

8. First Declension

Fill in the first declension case endings. Do it from memory if you want to show off! Use the Master Chart if you need it.

		Feminine (1st declension)
Singular	**Nominative** subject	α or η
	Genitive possession	
	Dative in, with, to, by	
	Accusative object	
Plural	**Nominative** subject	
	Genitive possession	
	Dative in, with, to, by	
	Accusative object	

Practice translating these sentences. Be sure to pay attention to the first declension endings to be sure to get the sentence in the right order. You can find the definitions on the next page.

I have listed them as you would find them in a Greek dictionary (called a "lexicon"). The lexicon will list:

1. The noun
2. The genitive ending
3. The article

The genitive ending tells us which declension to follow (first declension in this case).
The article tells us that that the noun is feminine (ἡ is the feminine article)

We will learn more about this in the next lesson.

Take a Hike! 27

Greek	English	Cognates
ἀγάπη, ης, ἡ	love	
ἀλήθεια, ας, ἡ	truth	
ἁμαρτία, ας, ἡ	sin	
βασιλεία, ας, ἡ	kingdom	A basilisk is a legendary reptile reputed to be king of serpents. (Harry Potter, anyone?)
δόξα, ης, ἡ	glory	A "doxology" is a word of praise.
ἐκκλησία, ας, ἡ	church	An ecclesiastic council is a gathering of church leaders.
ἐξουσία, ας, ἡ	authority	
φωνή, ῆς, ἡ	voice	A phonograph records sound.
γῆ, γῆς, ἡ	earth	Geology is the study of the earth.
ἡμέρα, ας, ἡ	day	
καρδία, ας, ἡ	heart	Cardiology is the study of the heart.
ὥρα, ας, ἡ	hour	¿Que hora es? is how you ask what time ("hour") it is in Spanish.
ψυχή, ῆς, ἡ	soul	Psychology is the science of the human soul.
ζωή, ῆς, ἡ	life	Zoology is the study of animal life.

(Phrases)

ἀγάπη ζωῆς

ἡμέρα δόξης

(Sentences)

1. ἡ ἐκκλησία ἔχει τὴν ἐξουσίαν τῆς βασιλείας.
   the   has   the   the

2. ἡ καρδία τῆς ἁμαρτίας μισεῖ ἀλήθειαν.
   The   *   hates

3. ζωήν τῇ γῇ ἡ ψυχή τῆς ἀγάπης συνάξει.
        the the   *   will bring

4. ἡ ἐκκλησία ἐμαρτύρησεν τῇ δόξῃ τῆς ὥρας.
   the   bore witness   the   the

5. ψύχας ἁμαρτίαι λύουσιν.
                         destroy

Take a Hike! 29

6. ἀγαπήσεις τὴν βασιλείαν τῇ καρδίᾳ.
   You must love   the   the

7. ἀλήθεια δίδωσιν δόξαν τῇ ψυχῇ.
              gives   the

8. ἡ ἐκκλησία κηρύσσει ζωήν τῇ γῇ.
   the   preaches   the

9 ἡ ψυχή γνώσεται τὴν ἡμέραν καὶ τὴν ὥραν.
  the   will know   the   and   the

10. φωνή επρχεται τῇ γῇ.
             goes out   the

9. Second Declension

Fill in the second declension, masculine and neuter case endings. Do it from memory if you can. Use the Master Chart if you need to.

		Masculine (2nd declension)	Neuter (2nd declension)
Singular	Nominative (subject)	ος	ον
	Genitive (possession)		
	Dative (in, with, to, by)		
	Accusative (object)		
Plural	Nominative (subject)		
	Genitive (possession)		
	Dative (in, with, to, by)		
	Accusative (object)		

Practice bringing order to the chaos by translating the following sentences. The definitions of the nouns are in the chart below.

Greek	English	Cognates
ἄγγελος, ου, ὁ	angel	angel
ἀδελφός, οῦ, ὁ	brother	Philadelphia is the city of brotherly love.
ἄνθρωπος, ου, ὁ	man	Anthropology is the study of man.
ἔργον, ου, τό	work	Ergonomics is the study of how to design a workplace so that it does not injure the body.
εὐαγγέλιον, ου, τό	gospel	In Greek, ευ means "good." An ἄγγελος is an angel or messenger. So ευ + αγγελιον = "good message" or good news.

Take a Hike! 31

Greek	English	Cognates
θεός, οῦ, ὁ	God	Theology is the study of God
ἱερόν, οῦ, τό	temple	
κόσμος, ου, ὁ	world	The cosmos is the world and universe
κύριος, ου, ὁ	Lord	
λόγος, ου, ὁ	word	
νόμος, ου, ὁ	law	
οὐρανός, οῦ, ὁ	heaven	
πρόσωπον, ου, τό	face	
τέκνον, ου, τό	child	

1. θεός ἀγάπᾳ τὸν κόσμον.
         loves   the

2. τὸν κόσμον θεός ἀγάπᾳ.
   the   loves

3. ὁ κόσμος θεόν ἀγάπᾳ.
   the   loves

4. ὁ κύριος ἐκήρυξεν τὸ εὐαγγέλιον ἀνθρώποις.
   the   preached   the

Take a Hike! 32

5. ἐκήρυξεν ὁ κύριος ἀνθρώποις τὸ εὐαγγέλιον τοῦ θεοῦ.
   preached the   the   *

6. τοὺς ἀγγέλους τοῦ οὐρανοῦ ὁ κύριος ἀγαπᾷ.
   the   *   the   loves

7. τεκνία ἐν οὐρανῷ ὄψονται τὸν πρόσωπον τοῦ θεοῦ.
                        will see   the   *

8. Τοῖς τέκνοις τῶν ἀνθρώπων ἐδόθη ὁ νόμος τοῦ κυρίου.
   the   *   was given the   the

* not translated

9. Τό πρόσωπον ἀδελφοῦ φέρει δόξαν τῷ κόσμῳ.
   the   brings glory the

10. ἄγγελοι κυκλεύουσιν τό ἱερόν.
                surround   the

11. ὁ θεὸς τοῦ οὐρανοῦ πέμπει ἀγγέλους τῷ κόσμῳ.
   the   sends   the

12. Ἄγγελοι ποιοῦσιν τὸ ἔργον τοῦ θεοῦ ἐν τῷ ἱερῷ.
              do   the   *   the

10. Third Declension

Fill in the third declension, masculine/feminine and neuter case endings. Do it from memory if you can. Use the Master Chart to help if you must.

Third Declension Case Endings

		Masc / Fem (3rd declension)	Neuter (3rd declension)
Singular	Nominative — subject	ς	—
	Genitive — possession		
	Dative — in, with, to, by		
	Accusative — object		
Plural	Nominative — subject		
	Genitive — possession		
	Dative — in, with, to, by		
	Accusative — object		

Translate the following sentences. The definitions of the words are given below.

Greek	English	Cognates
αἷμα, ατος, τό	blood	Hemoglobin carries oxygen in the blood.
ἀνήρ, ἀνδρός, ὁ	man	Anthropology is the study of man.
ἀρχιερεύς, έως, ὁ	chief priest	ἀρχή (first) + ἱερεύς (priest)
βασιλεύς, έως,* ὁ	king	
δύναμις, εως,* ἡ	power	dynamite
γυνή, γυναικός, ἡ	woman	A gynecologist is a women's doctor.

Take a Hike! 35

Greek	English	Cognates
ὄνομα, ατος, τό	name	
πατήρ, πατρός, ὁ	father	Your paternal grandmother is your grandmother on your father's side.
πίστις, εως,* ἡ	faith	Epistemology asks how we know what we know.
πνεῦμα, ατος, τό	spirit, wind	Pneumatic tools use pressurized air.
πόλις, εως,* ἡ	city	A politician is a ruler of a city or cities.
σῶμα, ατος, τό	body	Somatic illness is bodily illness (as opposed to mental illness).
χάρις, ιτος, ἡ	grace	The eucharist is a memorial supper in celebration of God's grace.
χείρ, χειρος, ἡ	hand	Chirography is the study of handwriting.

* some third declensions follow a slightly altered pattern. The full paradigm for the words with asterisks is on the next page. Third declension nouns are the least consistent. However, if you pay attention to patterns it is pretty easy to recognize the case in spite of their irregularities. Also, the article will help us immensely. We will learn it next.

πίστις, εως, ἡ (faith) (feminine)

Singular	Nominative (subject)	πίστις
	Genitive (possession)	πίστεως
	Dative (in, with, to, by)	πίστει
	Accusative (object)	πίστιν
Plural	Nominative (subject)	πίστεις
	Genitive (possession)	πίστεων
	Dative (in, with, to, by)	πίστεσιν
	Accusative (object)	πίστεις

πόλις, εως, ἡ (city) (feminine)

Singular	Nominative (subject)	πόλις
	Genitive (possession)	πόλεως
	Dative (in, with, to, by)	πόλει
	Accusative (object)	πόλιν
Plural	Nominative (subject)	πόλεις
	Genitive (possession)	πόλεων
	Dative (in, with, to, by)	πόλεσιν
	Accusative (object)	πόλεις

βασιλεύς, εως, ὁ (king) (masculine)

Singular	Nominative (subject)	βασιλεύς
	Genitive (possession)	βασιλέως
	Dative (in, with, to, by)	βασιλεῖ
	Accusative (object)	βασιλέα
Plural	Nominative (subject)	βασιλεῖς
	Genitive (possession)	βασιλέων
	Dative (in, with, to, by)	βασιλεῦσιν
	Accusative (object)	βασιλεῖς

1. χάρις ἔσωσεν τὸν πατέρα.
         saved   the

2. πίστις σῴζει ἄνδρας καὶ γυναῖκας τῇ δυνάμει τῆς χάριτος.
       saves   the   *

3. ὁ βασιλεύς βασιλεύει τὸν πόλιν[1] ἐν δυνάμει.
   the   rules   the   in

4. ἡ πόλις πληροῖ τῷ αἵματι τῶν πατέρων.
   the   is filled the   the

5. τὸ πνεῦμα[2] νικᾷ χάριτι.
   the   conquers

---

[1] This is an odd form of the accusative.

[2] This is nominative, neuter, singular. It is a ματ stem noun that follows the same pattern as ὄνομα. There is no ending in the nominative, so we would expect ὄνοματ. For some reason, Greeks did not like ending words with τ's so they dropped them, leaving ὄνομα. Ματ stem nouns are always third declension neuter and are very common.

Take a Hike!

6. ὁ πατήρ[1] ἐνέκρυψεν τὸ ὄνομα[2] τῆς γυναικός.
   the   concealed   the

7. ὁ βασιλεύς ἔχει αἷμα[3] ἐπὶ τάς χείρας αὐτοῦ.
   the   has   on   *   of him (= his)

8. αἷμα[4] δίδωσιν δύναμιν[5] τῷ σώματι.
         gives   the

9. ἡ πόλις πληροῖ τῷ αἵματι τῶν ἀρχιερέων.
   the   is filled the   *

10. χάρις οὐ ἔρχεται τῇ χειρὶ ἀνδρῶν.
        not   come the

---

[1] Another example of an odd nominative, masculine singular form. Are you seeing a pattern? Nominative masculine singular forms are often irregular. You can see the full paradigm for πατήρ on page 65 of the Mt Κοίνη grammar book.

[2] Accusative, neuter, singular. A ματ stem noun.

[3] Accusative, neuter, singular. A ματ stem noun.

[4] Here we go again. A ματ stem noun. Its form could be either nominative or accusative. You must decide from the context.

[5] Another odd form of the accusative, similar to πόλιν in question #3 above.

Camp Modifier

The Article and Adjectives

11. The Article

Questions

____ Articles must match the noun they modify in:
   a. Case, Number and Gender
   b. Declension
   c. Case and Number
   d. Number and Gender

____ Why are there twenty four forms of the article but only eight forms of every noun?
   a. Because articles are made of only a few letters.
   b. Because articles have to be able to be masculine *and* feminine *and* neuter.
   c. Because articles have more than four cases.
   d. There is no logical explanation.

Match the article with the noun it modifies.

___	τοῖς	1	λόγους
___	τῆς	2	τέκνον
___	τούς	3	ἡμερῆς
___	τῶν	4	πίστεων
___	τό	5	ἀδελφοῖς

Do yourself a favor: memorize the article!

- When you know the article, you will also know the first and second declension case endings.
- The article will save you when you do not recognize the case ending of a troublesome noun.

Practice filling out the article chart from memory. I have provided two charts so you can practice, practice, practice.

On this lesson's quiz, I will ask you a few general questions about the article, then ask you to fill in some holes in the article chart.

The Article

		M (2)	F (1)	N (2)
Singular	Nominative "the"			
Singular	Genitive "of the"			
Singular	Dative "to the"			
Singular	Accusative the			
Plural	Nominative "the"			
Plural	Genitive "of the"			
Plural	Dative "to the"			
Plural	Accusative "the"			

Take a Hike! 41

The Article

			M (2)	F (1)	N (2)
Singular	Nominative	"the"			
Singular	Genitive	"of the"			
Singular	Dative	"to the"			
Singular	Accusative	the			
Plural	Nominative	"the"			
Plural	Genitive	"of the"			
Plural	Dative	"to the"			
Plural	Accusative	"the"			

The Article

			M (2)	F (1)	N (2)
Singular	Nominative	"the"			
Singular	Genitive	"of the"			
Singular	Dative	"to the"			
Singular	Accusative	the			
Plural	Nominative	"the"			
Plural	Genitive	"of the"			
Plural	Dative	"to the"			
Plural	Accusative	"the"			

12. 2-1-2 Adjectives

Please provide the article and adjective endings in the table below. I did the nominative, masculine, singular for you. Do not worry about accents.

I realize this is a repetitive. But this kind of practice really helps to stick ideas in the brain. You may check your answers in the Mt. Κοίνη Grammar.

the good word / beginning / work

		Masculine (2nd declension)		Feminine (1st declension)		Neuter (2nd declension)
N	ος	ὁ ἀγαθος λογος — the good word	α..η	___ ἀγαθ__ ἀρχή — the good beginning	ον	___ ἀγαθ__ ἔργον — the good work
G	ου	___ ἀγαθ__ λόγου — of the good word	ας..ης	___ ἀγαθ__ ἀρχῆς — of the good beginning	ου	___ ἀγαθ__ ἔργου — of the good work
D	ῳ	___ ἀγαθ__ λόγῳ — to the good word	ᾳ..ῃ	___ ἀγαθ__ ἀρχῇ — to the good beginning	ῳ	___ ἀγαθ__ ἔργῳ — to the good work
A	ον	___ ἀγαθ__ λόγον — the good word	αν..ην	___ ἀγαθ__ ἀρχήν — the good beginning	ον	___ ἀγαθ__ ἔργον — the good work
N	οι	___ ἀγαθ__ λόγοι — the good words	αι	___ ἀγαθ__ ἀρχαί — the good beginnings	α	___ ἀγαθ__ ἔργα — the good works
G	ων	___ ἀγαθ__ λόγων — of the good words	ων	___ ἀγαθ__ ἀρχῶν	ων	___ ἀγαθ__ ἔργων — of the good works
D	οις	___ ἀγαθ__ λόγοις — to the good words	αις	___ ἀγαθ__ ἀρχαῖς	οις	___ ἀγαθ__ ἔργοις — to the good works
A	ους	___ ἀγαθ__ λόγους — the good words	ας	___ ἀγαθ__ ἀρχάς — the good beginnings	α	___ ἀγαθ__ ἔργα — the good works

On the next page, supply the correct form of the 2-1-2 adjective ἅγιος (holy) with the nouns and provide a translation. Don't worry about accents.

Remember, the adjective must match the noun in case, number and gender.

You will probably find this challenging. Do your best, then use the answers in the back to help.

All of the nouns were on the week 2 vocabulary list.

Take a Hike! 43

	Adjective (ἅγιος, ἁγία, ἅγιον)	Noun	Translation
1	ἁγίᾳ	ζωῇ	to a holy life
2		λόγους	
3		λογῶν	
4		ζωαῖς	
5		ἔργα	
6		δόξαι	
7		καρδία	
8		ἀγγέλοις	
9		ἐργοῦ	
10		ἐκκλησίαν	

The words below are trickier since they are third declension nouns. The endings of ἅγιος will not match the nouns they modify. ἅγιος is a 2-1-2 adjective but these nouns are 3rd declension. Remember: the adjective must match the noun it modifies in case, number & gender. **The declensions do not have to match.**

11		ἀνδρός	
12		ὀνόματι	
13		χάριτες	
14		βασιλέων	
15		πίστιν	

13. 3-1-3 Adjectives

Use the case endings chart to supply the case endings for the 3-1-3 adjective, πας.

		Masculine	Feminine	Neuter
Singular	n	πα	πασ	πα
	g	παντ	πασ	παντ
	d	παντ	πασ	παντ
	a	παντ	πασ	πα
Plural	n	παντ	πασ	παντ
	g	παντ	πασ	παντ
	d	πασ	πασ	πασ
	a	παντ	πασ	παντ

On the next page, supply the correct form of the 3-1-3 adjective πᾶς ("all" or "every") with the nouns and provide a translation. Don't worry about accents.

Remember: The adjective must match the noun in case, number and gender. It does not have to match in declension.

You may find this challenging. Do your best, then use the answer key if you get stuck.

Take a Hike! 45

You have seen all of these words on your vocabulary lists. You can look them up in the Vocabulary Whacker if you need to.

	Adjective (πάς, πάσα, πάν)	**Noun**	**Translation**
1	πασῃ	ζωῇ	to every life
2	παντας	λόγους	
3		νομῶν	
4		ψυχαῖς	
5		ἔργα	
6		ἡμέραι	
7		καρδία	
8		ἀγγέλοις	
9		εὐαγγελίου	
10		ἀλήθειαν	
	Note: The words below are third declension nouns		
11	παντος	ἀνδρός	
12		ὀνόματι	
13		χάριτες	
14		βασιλέων	
15		πίστιν	

Take a Hike! 46

The adjective "one" declines as follows. Since it only modifies singular subjects, there are no plural forms.

		Masculine	Feminine	Neuter
Singular	n	εἷς	μία	ἕν
	g	ἑνός	μιᾶς	ἑνός
	d	ἑνί	μιᾷ	ἑνί
	a	ἕνα	μίαν	ἕν

14. 2-2 & 3-3 Adjectives

Use the case ending chart to supply the case endings for the 2-2 adjective ἁμαρτωλός.

	Masculine Feminine	Neuter
n	ἁμαρτωλ	ἁμαρτωλ
g	ἁμαρτωλ	ἁμαρτωλ
d	ἁμαρτωλ	ἁμαρτωλ
a	ἁμαρτωλ	ἁμαρτωλ
n	ἁμαρτωλ	ἁμαρτωλ
g	ἁμαρτωλ	ἁμαρτωλ
d	ἁμαρτωλ	ἁμαρτωλ
a	ἁμαρτωλ	ἁμαρτωλ

Use the case ending chart to supply the case endings for the 3-3 adjective μείζων.

μείζων [3-3]

	(3) Masculine and (3) Feminine	(3) Neuter
n	μειζων	μειζον
g	μειζονος	μειζονος
d	μειζονι	μειζονι
a	μειζονα	μειζον
n	μειζονες	μειζονα
g	μειζονων	μειζονων
d	μειζοσι[ν]	μειζοσι[ν]
a	μειζονας	μειζονα

	Masculine Feminine	Neuter
n	μειζ	μειζον
g	μειζον	μειζον
d	μειζον	μειζον
a	μειζον	μειζον
n	μειζον	μειζον
g	μειζον	μειζον
d	μειζο	μειζο
a	μειζον	μειζον

Take a Hike! 49

Supply the correct form of the 2-2 adjective ἁμαρτωλός (sinful) or μείζων (greater) and provide a translation. Don't worry about accents.

Remember, the adjective must match the noun in case, number and gender. It does not have to match in declension.

You have seen all of these words on your vocabulary lists. Look them up in the Vocabulary Whacker if you need to.

ἁμαρτωλός [2-2]

	(2) Masculine and (2) Feminine	(2) Neuter
n	ἁμαρτωλος	ἁμαρτωλον
g	ἁμαρτωλου	ἁμαρτωλου
d	ἁμαρτωλῳ	ἁμαρτωλῳ
a	ἁμαρτωλον	ἁμαρτωλον
n	ἁμαρτωλοι	ἁμαρτωλα
g	ἁμαρτωλων	ἁμαρτωλων
d	ἁμαρτωλοις	ἁμαρτωλοις
a	ἁμαρτωλους	ἁμαρτωλα

μείζων [3-3]

	(3) Masculine and (3) Feminine	(3) Neuter
n	μειζων	μειζον
g	μειζονος	μειζονος
d	μειζονι	μειζονι
a	μειζονα	μειζον
n	μειζονες	μειζονα
g	μειζονων	μειζονων
d	μειζοσι[ν]	μειζοσι[ν]
a	μειζονας	μειζονα

	Adjective (ἁμαρτωλός, μείζων)	Noun	Translation
1 sinful	ἁμαρτωλῳ	ζωῇ	to a sinful life
2 greater	μειζονας	λόγους	greater words
3 sinful	ἁμαρτωλων	νομῶν	of sinful laws
4 greater	μειζοσι(ν)	ψυχαῖς	to greater souls
5 sinful	ἁμαρτωλα	ἔργα	sinful works
6 sinful	ἁμαρτωλοι	ἡμέραι	sinful days

ἁμαρτωλός [2-2]

	(2) Masculine and (2) Feminine	(2) Neuter
n	ἁμαρτωλος	ἁμαρτωλον
g	ἁμαρτωλου	ἁμαρτωλου
d	ἁμαρτωλῳ	ἁμαρτωλῳ
a	ἁμαρτωλον	ἁμαρτωλον
n	ἁμαρτωλοι	ἁμαρτωλα
g	ἁμαρτωλων	ἁμαρτωλων
d	ἁμαρτωλοις	ἁμαρτωλοις
a	ἁμαρτωλους	ἁμαρτωλα

μείζων [3-3]

	(3) Masculine and (3) Feminine	(3) Neuter
n	μειζων	μειζον
g	μειζονος	μειζονος
d	μειζονι	μειζονι
a	μειζονα	μειζον
n	μειζονες	μειζονα
g	μειζονων	μειζονων
d	μειζοσι[ν]	μειζοσι[ν]
a	μειζονας	μειζονα

	Adjective (ἁμαρτωλός, μείζων)	Noun	Translation
7 sinful		καρδία	
8 greater		ἄγγελοις	
9 greater		εὐαγγελίου	
10 greater		ἀλήθειαν	
Note: The words below are third declension nouns			
11 greater		ἀνδρός	
12 sinful		ὀνόματι	
13 greater		χάριτες	
14 sinful		βασιλέων	
15 greater		πίστιν	

Take a Hike! 51

τρεῖς is a 3-3 adjective that declines as follows. There are no singular forms of τρεῖς because it only modifies plural subjects.

	Masculine Femine	Neuter
n	τρεῖς	τρία
g	τριῶν	τριῶν
d	τρισίν	τρισίν
a	τρεῖς	τρία

15. Adjective Usage

1. Match the adjective with its definition.

   ___ Attributive Adjective   1   involves some form of "to be"

   ___ Substantival Adjective   2   "attributes" some quality to a noun

   ___ Predicate Adjective   3   "stands in" for an implied noun.

2. In the following two paragraphs on the next page,

   underline the attributive adjectives,

   put a box around the substantival adjectives, and

   circle the predicate adjectives.

Greek is difficult. When you start, you think it will be easy, but as you go along you find out that it is hard. Hopefully, you will have a skilled teacher who can guide you through the murky waters. Don't give up! The persistent will reap a great reward.

Jesus said that the meek would inherit the earth. All have heard this saying but few believe it to be true. Instead, it seems like greedy, immoral people tend to get ahead in our troubled world. This is terrible!

3. ____ Which form of the Greek adjectives never has the article?
   a. attributive
   b. substantival
   c. predicate

Pronoun Point

Pronouns!

GREEK FOR EVERYONE

16. First & Second Person Pronouns

Complete the following table *in English*.

	Singular	Plural
First Person I We	N: G: D: A:	N: G: D: A:
Second Person You You	N: G: D: A:	N: G: D: A:

Underline the first and second person pronouns in this story from my childhood.

Wild Accusations

My mom and dad were standing beside me on the gravel road that ran past our house, happily watching my little sister, Jane. She was wobbling her way down a hill on a shiny pink bicycle, experiencing for the first time the wonder of unassisted balance and motion on two wheels.

Newborn skills are fragile. As the bike rolled down the hill it gained dangerous speed. Playful wobbling turned into desperate zigs and zags. Jane's path became as frantic as the look on her face. Faster and faster she went, her control diminishing as her velocity increased. A final desperate zag sent her smashing squarely into me. She erupted in an instinctive and outraged, "MOOOOOREEEEEE!"

I confess that I used to delight in provoking this reaction from my little sister. But on this occasion I was as innocent as the mailbox on the road beside me. As my sister and I picked ourselves up out of the gravel, we heard mom and dad in the background, laughing uproariously at the wild ride and even wilder accusation.

I have been feeling a lot like Jane on that bike lately. As I wobble down life's road, I keep gaining speed, losing control and plowing into things. My instinct is to blame innocent bystanders.

I am slowly learning to face the facts: The only hands doing any steering are the ones attached to my own arms and if I ever want to learn to ride I must stop complaining about everyone else and take responsibility for my own collisions.

Supply English translations for the first and second person Greek pronouns.

1st Person		
Singular	Nom	ἐγώ
	Gen	μου ἐμοῦ
	Dat	μοι ἐμοί
	Acc	με ἐμέ
Plural	Nom	ἡμεῖς
	Gen	ἡμῶν
	Dat	ἡμῖν
	Acc	ἡμᾶς

2nd Person		
Singular	Nom	σύ
	Gen	σου σοῦ
	Dat	σοι σοί
	Acc	σε σέ
Plural	Nom	ὑμεῖς
	Gen	ὑμῶν
	Dat	ὑμῖν
	Acc	ὑμᾶς

Match the pronoun with its definition.

___ μοι   1 your (plural)

___ σοι   2 you

___ ὑμῶν   3 us

___ ἡμῶν   4 I

___ σύ   5 our (plural)

___ ὑμῖν   6 to me

___ ἡμᾶς   7 to you (plural)

___ ἐγώ   8 to you (singular)

Take a Hike! 58

Underline the first and second person pronouns in the following text. Do not worry that you cannot yet translate this. You will be able to soon!

15.1 Ἐγώ εἰμι ἡ ἄμπελος ἡ ἀληθινή, καὶ ὁ πατήρ μου ὁ γεωργός ἐστιν· 2 πᾶν κλῆμα ἐν ἐμοὶ μὴ φέρον καρπὸν αἴρει αὐτό, καὶ πᾶν τὸ καρπὸν φέρον καθαίρει αὐτὸ ἵνα καρπὸν πλείονα φέρῃ. 3 ἤδη ὑμεῖς καθαροί ἐστε διὰ τὸν λόγον ὃν λελάληκα ὑμῖν· 4 μείνατε ἐν ἐμοί, κἀγὼ ἐν ὑμῖν. καθὼς τὸ κλῆμα οὐ δύναται καρπὸν φέρειν ἀφ' ἑαυτοῦ ἐὰν μὴ μένῃ ἐν τῇ ἀμπέλῳ, οὕτως οὐδὲ ὑμεῖς ἐὰν μὴ ἐν ἐμοὶ μένητε. 5 ἐγώ εἰμι ἡ ἄμπελος, ὑμεῖς τὰ κλήματα. ὁ μένων ἐν ἐμοὶ κἀγὼ ἐν αὐτῷ οὗτος φέρει καρπὸν πολύν, ὅτι χωρὶς ἐμοῦ οὐ δύνασθε ποιεῖν οὐδέν. 6 ἐὰν μή τις μένῃ ἐν ἐμοί, ἐβλήθη ἔξω ὡς τὸ κλῆμα καὶ ἐξηράνθη, καὶ συνάγουσιν αὐτὰ καὶ εἰς τὸ πῦρ βάλλουσιν καὶ καίεται. 7 ἐὰν μείνητε ἐν ἐμοὶ καὶ τὰ ῥήματά μου ἐν ὑμῖν μείνῃ, ὃ ἐὰν θέλητε αἰτήσασθε καὶ γενήσεται ὑμῖν· 8 ἐν τούτῳ ἐδοξάσθη ὁ πατήρ μου ἵνα καρπὸν πολὺν φέρητε καὶ γένησθε ἐμοὶ μαθηταί. 9 καθὼς ἠγάπησέν με ὁ πατήρ, κἀγὼ ὑμᾶς ἠγάπησα, μείνατε ἐν τῇ ἀγάπῃ τῇ ἐμῇ. 10 ἐὰν τὰς ἐντολάς μου τηρήσητε, μενεῖτε ἐν τῇ ἀγάπῃ μου, καθὼς ἐγὼ τὰς ἐντολὰς τοῦ πατρός μου τετήρηκα καὶ μένω αὐτοῦ ἐν τῇ ἀγάπῃ.

17. Third Person Pronouns

Complete the following table *in English*.

	Singular	Plural
Third Person He-She-It They	N: G: D: A:	N: G: D: A:

Please underline the third person pronouns in the following essay.

The Rider

I am a sucker for a John Wayne movie. For one thing, I like a world in which good and evil are clearly identified by the color of hats and horses. But also, I like justice. When the Duke rides onto the screen, I rest assured that justice follows close behind. Good and evil will soon be repaid in exact proportion to their magnitude. How could I not cheer?

The first time I saw the trailer for the remake of True Grit I was offended. Why remake a masterpiece? I would have gladly joined a posse to bring the Coen brothers in and lock them up if I had been asked. But having watched the remake four times now, I have no choice but to declare myself a fan.

Good and evil are much more complicated in the new version. Recoil from the shot that brings justice to her father's murderer sends Maddie sprawling into a pit. In that blackness, serpents slither from the heart of a dead man and latch onto her hand. Maddie winds up a spinster, walking around with a scowl and half an arm missing. Justice is messy business.

Good and evil are not hard to tell apart; they are just hard to take apart. Our world and our souls are fields of wheat sown with tares. It is hard to distinguish the good from the bad by their surface appearance, and hidden roots are hopelessly tangled. Our shameful treatment of a truly good man who rode into town on a donkey should give us pause to question our wisdom as judges.

In Saint John's vision of the apocalypse, the same rider will appear again on the human scene, this time not on a donkey but on a white horse with the sword of justice drawn. I cannot help but cheer for justice. But if John has it right and I must one day face that rider, I know without question that cry of my heart will not be for justice but for mercy.

Please supply the English translations for the Greek third person pronoun.

		M (2)	F (1)	N (2)
Singular	Nom	αὐτός	αὐτή	αὐτό
	Gen	αὐτοῦ	αὐτῆς	αὐτοῦ
	Dat	αὐτῷ	αὐτῇ	αὐτῷ
	Acc	αὐτόν	αὐτήν	αὐτό
Plural	Nom	αὐτοί	αὐταί	αὐτά
	Gen	αὐτῶν	αὐτῶν	αὐτῶν
	Dat	αὐτοῖς	αὐταῖς	αὐτοῖς
	Acc	αὐτούς	αὐτάς	αὐτά

Underline the third person pronouns in the following text. Do not worry that you cannot yet translate this. You will be able to soon!

11.1 Ἦν δέ τις ἀσθενῶν, Λάζαρος ἀπὸ Βηθανίας ἐκ τῆς κώμης Μαρίας καὶ Μάρθας τῆς ἀδελφῆς αὐτῆς. 2 ἦν δὲ Μαριὰμ ἡ ἀλείψασα τὸν κύριον μύρῳ καὶ ἐκμάξασα τοὺς πόδας αὐτοῦ ταῖς θριξὶν αὐτῆς, ἧς ὁ ἀδελφὸς Λάζαρος ἠσθένει. 3 ἀπέστειλαν οὖν αἱ ἀδελφαὶ πρὸς αὐτὸν λέγουσαι· Κύριε, ἴδε ὃν φιλεῖς ἀσθενεῖ. 4 ἀκούσας δὲ ὁ Ἰησοῦς εἶπεν· Αὕτη ἡ ἀσθένεια οὐκ ἔστιν πρὸς θάνατον ἀλλ' ὑπὲρ τῆς δόξης τοῦ θεοῦ ἵνα δοξασθῇ ὁ υἱὸς τοῦ θεοῦ δι' αὐτῆς. 5 ἠγάπα δὲ ὁ Ἰησοῦς

τὴν Μάρθαν καὶ τὴν ἀδελφὴν αὐτῆς καὶ τὸν Λάζαρον.
⁶ ὡς οὖν ἤκουσεν ὅτι ἀσθενεῖ, τότε μὲν ἔμεινεν ἐν ᾧ ἦν τόπῳ δύο ἡμέρας·

Match the underlined English pronoun with the corresponding Greek pronoun.

___ I am sure <u>he</u> is the one.   1 αὐτόν

___ Give this candy <u>to her</u>.   2 ἡμᾶς

___ They are making life difficult for <u>us</u>.   3 αὐτοῖς

___ Give my best <u>to them</u>.   4 αὐτή

___ I find <u>him</u> a very likeable fellow.   5 αὐτός

___ <u>She</u> is my hero.   6 αὐτῇ

___ Where do you hide <u>it</u>?   7 αὐτό

18. Relative Pronouns

Which of the following sentences contain a relative pronoun?

- ☐ The dog who lives at our house is spoiled
- ☐ Whose dog is this?
- ☐ To whom do I owe the honor?
- ☐ This is the woman to whom we owe the honor

Underline the relative clauses in the two sentences above which contain a relative pronoun.

Practice filling in the relative pronouns. Do as much as possible from memory. This is a great review of the 2-1-2 case endings.

Relative Pronoun

		M (2)	F (1)	N (2)
Singular	Nom	who	who	which
	Gen	of whom	of whom	of which
	Dat	to whom	to whom	to which
	Acc	whom	whom	which
Plural	Nom	who	who	which
	Gen	of whom	of whom	of which
	Dat	to whom	to whom	to which
	Acc	whom	whom	which

On the next page, please write a smooth translation of the verse, being sure to translate the relative pronoun correctly. I have filled in words you have not yet met. You will need to translate some first, second, and third person pronouns.

Take a Hike! 64

1. ἐρωτῶ περὶ ὧν δέδωκάς μοι.
   I am asking concerning   you have given

2. ὁ ἀστὴρ ὃν εἶδον ἐν τῇ ἀνατολῇ προῆγεν
   The   star   they saw   East   (it) led

   αὐτούς.

3. καὶ ὃς οὐ λαμβάνει τὸν σταυρὸν οὐκ ἔστιν
                not (he) takes up   cross   not   he is

   μου ἄξιος.
         worthy

4. Ὃς ἔχει ὦτα ἀκούειν ἀκουέτω.
      (he) has   ears   to hear   let him hear!

5. οὗτός ἐστιν ὁ χριστός, ὁ Ἰησοῦς ὃν ἐγὼ
   This   (it) is the Christ   *   Jesus

   καταγγέλλω ὑμῖν.
   (I) announce

6. ὅστις οὐκ ἔχει, καὶ ὃ ἔχει ἀρθήσεται ἀπ'
   Whoever not (he) has even he has (it) will be taken

   αὐτοῦ.

7. πέντε ἄνδρας ἔσχες, καὶ νῦν ὃν ἔχεις οὐκ
   Five husbands you have had   now   you have   not

   ἔστιν σου ἀνήρ
   he is   husband.

8. Πῶς ἐπικαλέσωνται εἰς ὃν οὐκ ἐπίστευσαν;
   How   shall they call   not   they believed

19. Interrogative and Indefinite Pronouns

Which pronoun always has an accent on the first syllable?

☐ The interrogative pronoun
☐ The indefinite pronoun

Supply the Greek pronouns.

	Relative	Interrogative	Indefinite
English	who, which	who? which? what?	someone something anyone anything
Greek			

Write out the chart of the interrogative and indefinite pronouns. Be sure to put an accent on the first syllable of the interrogative pronouns. This is also great practice for your third declension case endings.

Interrogative Pronoun

		M / F (3)	N (3)
Singular	Nom	who? what?	which? what?
	Gen	of whom? of what?	of which? of what?
	Dat	to whom? to what?	to which? to what?
	Acc	whom? what?	which? what?
Plural	Nom	who? what?	which? what?
	Gen	of whom? of what?	of which? of what?
	Dat	to whom? to what?	to which? to what?
	Acc	whom? what?	which? what?

Indefinite Pronoun

		M / F (3)	N (3)
Singular	Nom	someone something	something
	Gen	of someone of something	of something
	Dat	to someone to something	to something
	Acc	someone something	something
Plural	Nom	someone something	something
	Gen	of someone of something	of something
	Dat	to someone to something	to something
	Acc	someone something	something

Take a Hike! 67

1. τίς ὑπέδειξεν ὑμῖν φυγεῖν ἀπὸ τῆς
       warned   you   to flee

   μελλούσης ὀργῆς;
     coming   wrath

2. τίς σοι ἔδωκεν τὴν ἐξουσίαν ταύτην;
       gave   *   authority   this

3. Τίς ἐστιν οὗτος ὃς λαλεῖ βλασφημίας;[1]
       is   this   speaks

4. Τίνα θέλετε ἀπολύσω ὑμῖν;
     do you want   me to release

---

[1] Sound it out!

5. Τί δοκεῖς, Σίμων;[1]
     do you think

6. οὐ χρείαν εἶχεν ἵνα τις μαρτυρήσῃ περὶ τοῦ
   No   need   he had for   to bear witness

   ἀνθρώπου.

7. ἀλλὰ εἰσὶν ἐξ ὑμῶν τινες οἳ οὐ πιστεύουσιν.[2]
   But   there are   who not   they believe

8. ἀσθενεῖ τις ἐν ὑμῖν;
   is weak

9. ἦν τις βασιλικὸς οὗ ὁ υἱὸς ἠσθένει.
   there was   king   whose   son   he was weak

---

[1] Sound it out!

[2] 7-9 are challenging. Don't feel stupid! It takes a while to get used to the indefinite pronoun. Use the answer key and see if you can see what is going on.

Take a Hike! 69

20. Demonstrative and Reflexive Pronouns

The demonstrative pronouns follow what pattern of declension? _____

Near demonstrative pronouns are easy to recognize because they always begin with a _____ breathing or a ____.

Far demonstrative pronouns always begin with _____.

Match the English pronoun with its type.

___ **this**   1 far demonstrative pronoun (singular)

___ **these**   2 near demonstrative pronoun (plural)

___ **that**   3 near demonstrative pronoun (singular)

___ **those**   4 far demonstrative pronoun (plural)

Match the Greek pronoun with its type.

___ **ἐκείνους**   1 far demonstrative pronoun (singular)

___ **οὗτοι**   2 near demonstrative pronoun (plural)

___ **τοῦτο**   3 near demonstrative pronoun (singular)

___ **ἐκείνη**   4 far demonstrative pronoun (plural)

Take a Hike! 70

Fill in the English translations for the near demonstrative pronoun.

		Near Demonstrative Pronoun		
		M (2)	F (1)	N (2)
Singular	Nom	οὗτος	αὕτη	τοῦτο
	Gen	τούτου	ταύτης	τούτου
	Dat	τούτῳ	ταύτῃ	τούτῳ
	Acc	τοῦτον	ταύτην	τοῦτο
Plural	Nom	οὗτοι	αὗται	ταῦτα
	Gen	τούτων	τούτων	τούτων
	Dat	τούτοις	ταύταις	τούτοις
	Acc	τούτους	ταύτας	ταῦτα

Practice filling in the endings of the far demonstrative pronoun. This is great practice for nailing the 2-1-2 pattern. See if you can do it by memory.

		Far Demonstrative Pronoun		
		M (2)	F (1)	N (2)
Singular	Nom	ἐκειν___ that	ἐκειν___ that	ἐκειν___ that
	Gen	ἐκειν___ of that	ἐκειν___ of that	ἐκειν___ of that
	Dat	ἐκειν___ to that	ἐκειν___ to that	ἐκειν___ to that
	Acc	ἐκειν___ that	ἐκειν___ that	ἐκειν___ that
Plural	Nom	ἐκειν___ those	ἐκειν___ those	ἐκειν___ those
	Gen	ἐκειν___ of those	ἐκειν___ of those	ἐκειν___ of those
	Dat	ἐκειν___ to those	ἐκειν___ to those	ἐκειν___ to those
	Acc	ἐκειν___ those	ἐκειν___ those	ἐκειν___ those

Take a Hike! 71

The reflexive pronouns follow the _____ pattern of declension.

Match the first, second, and third person reflexive pronoun with the clue used to distinguish it.

___ First Person (myself, ourselves)

___ Second Person (yourself, yourselves)

___ Third Person (himself, herself, itself themselves)

1 ἑ

2 ἐμ

3 σε

Match the reflexive pronoun with its translation.

___ ἐμαυτοῦ

___ ἑαυτῷ

___ ἑαυτά

___ ἐμαυτούς

___ ἑαυταῖς

___ σεαυτῆς

___ ἑαυτῶν

___ σεαυτόν

1 themselves
2 ourselves
3 to himself, itself
4 to themselves
5 of myself
6 yourself
7 of themselves
8 of yourself

Translate.

1. δευτέρα αὕτη· Ἀγαπήσεις τὸν πλησίον σου ὡς
   The second (is)   You shall love   the   neighbor   as

   σεαυτόν.

2. ἐρεῖτέ μοι τὴν παραβολὴν[1] ταύτην· Ἰατρέ,
   You will say   Physician

   θεράπευσον σεαυτόν·
   heal

---

[1] Sound it out.

Valley of the Verbs

GREEK
FOR EVERYONE

21. Tense, Voice, Mood, Person, Number

See if you can fill out the options from memory.

Tense	Voice	Mood	Person	Number
		(**P**articiple)		
		(I**N**finitive)		

Match the sentence with the correct <u>person and number</u>.

____ I love her!   1   third person plural

____ They will come later   2   third person singular

____ You (all) are making me tired.   3   first person singular

____ She will come someday.   4   first person plural

____ We will learn this yet!   5   second person plural

Match the sentence with the proper <u>voice</u>.

____ I ate the apple.   1   middle

____ I was eaten by an apple!   2   active

____ I ate an apple for myself.   3   passive

Match the sentence with the proper <u>mood</u>.

____ I hope we finish this one day.   1 indicative

____ Come inside!   2 imperative

____ It is getting cold outside.   3 subjunctive

Match the <u>tense</u> with its meaning.

____ ongoing aspect, past time   1 Present

____ undefined aspect, past time   2 Imperfect

____ event in past with ongoing effects   3 Future

____ undefined or ongoing aspect, present time   4 Aorist

____ undefined aspect, future time   5 Perfect

Match the sentence with the Greek tense that best represents the action of the verb.

____ I <u>am eating</u> Ice cream.   1 Present

____ I <u>slept</u>.   2 Imperfect

____ It <u>is written</u>.   3 Future

____ I <u>will mow</u> the lawn later today.   4 Aorist

____ I <u>was being chased</u> by bees!   5 Perfect

22. Personal Endings

Match the first person singular endings with their translation.

___ ω   1   I am being...

___ ομαι   2   I was...

___ ον   3   I was being...

___ ομην   4   I am...

Match the third person singular endings with their translation

___ ει   1   he/she/it was…

___ εται   2   he/she/it is being

___ ε(ν)   3   he/she/it is...

___ ετο   4   he/she/it was being...

Translate the following Greek sentences, paying close attention to the personal endings.

Primary Active Endings

1. πιστεύω τὸν θεόν.

2. βλέπομεν τὴν συναγωγήν.

3. διδάσκει τοὺς μαθητάς[1].

---

[1] Remember that this is an odd first declension masculine noun.

Take a Hike! 78

Primary Middle/Passive
(translate as passive)

4. διδασκόμεθα τὴν ἀλήθειαν.

5. βλέπομαι ἐν τῇ οἰκίᾳ.

6. διδάσκῃ περὶ τοῦ εὐαγγελίου.

Secondary Active

7. ἐπίστευες τὴν ἀλήθειαν.

8. ἐπίστευον ἐν τῇ βασιλείᾳ.

9. ἔβλεπομεν τὴν θάλασσην.

Secondary Middle/Passive
(translate as passive)

10. Ἰησους ἐκηρύσσετο τοῖς ἔθνεσιν.

11. Ἰησους ἐπέμπετο εἰς τὸν κόσμον.

12. τοὺς ἱεροὺς ἐλύοντο ὑπ' ἀνθρώπων.

23. Contract Verbs

Practice recognizing shapes.

Use the personal ending chart to see if you can match the contract verb with its translation. (These examples use only the primary endings.)

		Active (do the action)	Middle/Passive (receive the action)
Primary (present & future time)	(1s) I	ω	ομαι
	(2s) you	εις	η
	(3s) he/she/it	ει	εται
	(1p) we	ομεν	ομεθα
	(2p) you (all)	ετε	εσθε
	(3p) they	ουσι(ν)	ονται

___ ἀγαπῶμαι 1 We are making

___ ἀγαπᾷς 2 He is making

___ ἀγαπῶνται 3 They are making

___ ποιεῖ 4 You are filling

___ ποιοῦμεν 5 I am being loved

___ ποιοῦσι(ν) 6 You (all) are filling

___ πληροῖς 7 You are loving

___ πληροῦμαι 8 We are being filled

___ πληρούμεθα 9 They are being loved

___ πληροῦτε 10 I am being filled

ἀγαπάω means I love
ποιέω means I make (or do)
πληρόω means I fill

24. Regular Roots and Stems

Match the clues with the proper tense.

Tense		Clues
Present λύω _____	1	augment, present tense stem, secondary endings
Imperfect ἔλυον _____	2	reduplication, κ, primary active endings
Future λύσω _____	3	augment, σα, secondary endings
Aorist ἔλυσα _____	4	augment, θη, secondary active endings
Perfect Active λέλυκα _____	5	θης, primary m/p endings
Perfect Middle/Passive λέλυμαι _____	6	Present tense stem (lexical form), primary endings
Aorist Passive ἐλύθην _____	7	reduplication, no κ, no connecting vowel, primary middle/passive endings
Future Passive λυθήσομαι _____	8	σ before primary endings

Match the form of πιστεύω with its translation. Remember to look for the clues.
(This is challenging. Don't despair if you find it difficult!)

3	ἐπίστευον	1	We are being believed (or we are believed)
7	πεπίστευκεν	2	You were believed
8	πιστεύσετε	3	I (or they) were believing
4	πιστευθησόμεθα	4	We will be believed
2	ἐπίστευθης	5	I believed
1	πιστεύομεθα	6	They have come to be believed
6	πεπίστευνται	7	He/She/It has come to believe
5	ἐπίστευσα	8	You (all) will believe

Take a Hike! 81

25. Adverbs

In the following sentences, please circle the adverb and underline the verb it modifies.

- I have to admit that I *prepared* this lesson (reluctantly).
- The problem is that adverbs *are* (not) difficult.
- Once you learn to see them you *identify* them (easily).
- I *thought* about skipping this lesson (again).
- However, I *realized* that some of you *study* (diligently).
- You would *be* (annoyed) not to study every part of speech.
- So I (busily) *prepared* the video, *wrote* the grammar, and *updated* the workbook.
- I hope you will (not) *be* disappointed that it is (so) easy!

The Labyrinth

26. Liquid Verbs

Here is a list of some liquid verbs used more than fifty times in the New Testament. Circle the liquid consonant in each verb.

Greek	English	Cognates & Memory Aids
Liquid Verbs		
αἴρω	I take up, take away	An aeroplane takes you up, up, and away!
ἀναβαίνω	I go up	
ἀποκτείνω	I kill	
ἀποστέλλω	I send	Apostles are sent with a message.
βάλλω	I throw, put	Balls are thrown.
ἐγείρω	I raise up	
ἐκβάλλω	I cast out	
κρίνω	I judge, decide	Critics are often judgmental.
μέλλω	I am about to	
μένω	I remain, abide	Permanent things remain.
πίνω	I drink	Potions are drunk.
φέρω	I carry or bear	Freight is carried by trucks. Ferries are ships that carry cargo on water.
χαίρω	I rejoice	

Here are some liquid verbs in context. Underline the liquid consonant and translate the following sentences.

1. Ἐκ τοῦ στόματός σου κρίνῶ σε.

2. πῶς κρινεῖ ὁ θεὸς τὸν κόσμον;
   how

3. ἐν δικαιοσύνῃ κρίνεῖ καὶ πολεμσεῖ.[1]
                                           make war

4. οὐ ἔκρινά.

5. ἔκρινεν τὴν πόρνην τὴν μεγάλην.
                   prostitute

6. ὁ ὄχλος ἔμεινεν.
      crowd

---

[1] This is an epsilon contract verb: πολεμέω.

7. κἀγὼ αὐτὸν ἀρῶ.[1]

8. αὐτὸς ἔμεινεν ἐν τῇ Γαλιλαίᾳ.

9. ἐμείναμεν ἡμέραν μίαν παρ' αὐτοῖς.

10. ἀποστελῶ[2] αὐτοὺς λιμὸν καὶ θάνατον.
    famine

---

[1] Remember that vowels can shift around. This verb is in the Vocabulary Whacker. Look under "α."

[2] In this case, the future form drops a λ. Get used to these kinds of little changes. We are looking at the MAJOR patterns, not becoming obsessed by little details.

27. Second Aorists

Here is a list of some second aorists used more than 50 times in the New Testament. Notice that almost all of them end in ον (rather than σα).

Second Aorists

Lexical Form		2nd Aorist		Clues
ἀπέρχομαι	I depart	ἀπῆλθον	I departed	
ἀποθνήσκω	I die	ἀπέθανον	I died	
βάλλω	I throw	ἔβαλον	I threw	
γίνομαι	I am, become	ἐγενόμην	I was, became	
γινώσκω	I know	ἔγνων	I knew	Gnostics claim to know secrets of the universe.
εἰσέρχομαι	I go into	εἰσῆλθον	I went into	
ἐκβάλλω	I cast out	ἐξέβαλον	I cast out	
ἐξέρχομαι	I go out	ἐξῆλθον	I went out	
ἔρχομαι	I come (go)	ἦλθον	I came (went)	
ἐσθίω	I eat	ἔφαγον	I ate	
εὑρίσκω	I find	εὗρον	I found	Eureka! I found it! (Archimedes)
ἔχω	I have	ἔσχον	I had	
καταβαίνω	I go down	κατέβην	I went down	
λαμβάνω	I take	ἔλαβον	I took	
λέγω ἐρῶ, εἶπον, εἴρηκα, εἴρημαι, ἐρρέθην	I say, speak	εἶπον	I said, spoke	A monologue involves words said by a single person.
ὁράω ὄψομαι, εἶδον, ἑώρακα, *, ὤφθην	I see	εἶδον	I saw	A panoramic view sees all. (Παν means "all.")
πίνω	I drink	ἔπιον	I drank	Potions are drunk.
πίπτω	I fall	ἔπεσον	I fell	
προσέρχομαι	I come to	προσῆλθον	I came to	
συνάγω	I gather together	συνήγαγον	I gathered together	Jewish people gather together in synagogues.

Using the list of second aorists on the previous page, translate the following sentences.

1. ἦλθον δὲ οἱ δύο ἄγγελοι εἰς Σοδομα.
   (sound it out!)

2. ἦλθεν ὁ θεὸς πρὸς Βαλααμ νυκτὸς.[1]
   (sound it out!)   by night

3. ἔλαβεν κύριος ὁ θεὸς τὸν ἄνθρωπον, ὃν ἔπλασεν.
   he formed

---

[1] This is an example of how the genitive can be used to show time. "by night"

4. καὶ συνήγαγεν αὐτοὺς εἰς τὸν τόπον τὸν καλούμενον Ἑβραϊστὶ Ἁρμαγεδών.
                      called   in Hebrew   (sound it out!)

5. ὁμολογήσω αὐτοῖς ὅτι Οὐδέποτε[1] ἔγνων ὑμᾶς.
   I will say   never

6. εἶπεν δὲ πρὸς αὐτὸν ὁ ἄγγελος· Μὴ φοβοῦ, Ζαχαρία.
                                       (do) not fear
(sound it out!)

---

[1] This is a VERY strong way to say "never." It means "not at any time!"

28. Deponents

Here is a list of deponent verbs used more than 50 times in the New Testament. Notice that they end in ομαι rather than ω.

Deponent Verbs (present)		
ἀπέρχομαι	I depart	
ἀποκρίνομαι	I answer	
ἄρχομαι (ἄρχω means "I rule")	I begin	
ἀσπάζομαι	I greet, salute	
γίνομαι	I am, become	
δέχομαι	I receive	
δύναμαι	I am able, powerful	Dynamite gets the job done.
εἰσέρχομαι	I go into	
ἐξέρχομαι	I go out	We go out through the exit.
ἔρχομαι	I come (go)	
κάθημαι	I sit	
πορεύομαι	I go, proceed, live	
προσέρχομαι	I come to	
προσεύχομαι	I pray	

Using the personal endings chart, translate the following sentences (which contain deponent verbs).

		Personal Endings	
		Active (do the action)	**Middle/Passive** (receive the action)
Primary (present & future time)	(1s) I	ω	ομαι
	(2s) you	εις	η
	(3s) he/she/it	ει	εται
	(1p) we	ομεν	ομεθα
	(2p) you (all)	ετε	εσθε
	(3p) they	ουσι(ν)	ονται
Secondary (past time)	(1s) I	ον	ομην
	(2s) you	ες	ου
	(3s) he/she/it	ε(ν)	ετο
	(1p) we	ομεν	ομεθα
	(2p) you (all)	ετε	εσθε
	(3p) they	ον	οντο

Present Tense

1. ἔρχεται εἰς τὰ ὅρια τῆς Ἰουδαίας.
                         regions

2. ἔρχονται εἰς χωρίον οὗ τὸ ὄνομα Γεθσημανί.
                     place   (sound it out!)

3. Οὐκ ἀφήσω ὑμᾶς ὀρφανούς, ἔρχομαι πρὸς ὑμᾶς.
         I will leave   (orphans)

4. μετὰ δύο ἡμέρας τὸ πάσχα γίνεται.
   (after)

5. δύναται ὁ θεὸς ἐκ τῶν λίθων τούτων ἐγεῖραι τέκνα τῷ Ἀβραάμ.
   (to raise up)

6. Πιστεύετε ὅτι δύναμαι τοῦτο ποιῆσαι;[1]
   (to do)

7. Οὐκ ἀποκρίνῃ οὐδέν;

8. προσευχόμεθα πάντοτε περὶ ὑμῶν.
   (always)

---

[1] Don't forget to pay attention to punctuation!

Imperfect Tense

9. ἤρχοντο πρὸς αὐτόν.

10. πᾶς ὁ ὄχλος ἤρχετο πρὸς αὐτόν, καὶ
    all   the crowd

    ἐδίδασκεν[1] αὐτούς.
    he was teaching

11. ἔχοντες ἀσθενείας προσήρχοντο καὶ
    Those who were sick

    ἐθεραπεύοντο.[2]
    they were being healed

---

[1] Do you see how διδάσκω was modified to become imperfect? It was augmented and the secondary active ending was added.

[2] θεραπεύω means "I heal." Very therapeutic, right? Do you see how this verb was augmented and the secondary middle/passive ending was added to make it imperfect? "they were being healed"

29. Principal Parts

The best thing you can do to apply this lesson is spend some time staring lovingly at the Principal parts chart.

Look up and down each column until you see the following patterns in the six stems.

The Present Tense Stem

★ All of the white boxes end in ω. These are regular.

★ The green boxes are contract verbs. There is always an α, ε, or ο before the ω.

★ The yellow boxes are deponent. Most of them end in ομαι.

The Future Tense Stem

★ Notice the sigma before the personal endings. Sometimes it is hidden because of a collision of consonants (the square of stops). Κράξω and πέμψω are examples of this.

★ In the blue boxes (liquid futures), there is a λ, μ, ν or ρ and there is no sigma.

★ In the green boxes (contract verbs), the contract vowel lengthens before the sigma.

★ The yellow boxes are future middle deponent. They are middle in form but active in meaning. Notice that there are some verbs which are not deponent in the present tense but are deponent in the future (ἐσθίω and πίνω for example).

The Aorist Tense Stem

★ Look for the σα. Notice how in the white boxes it is easy to see unless it is buried in a collision of consonants (square of stops again). Ἀνέῳξα and ἔβλεψα are examples of this.

★ Study the different ways that the verbs are augmented.

★ In the blue boxes (liquid aorists), there is a λ, μ, ν or ρ and there is no sigma, only an alpha.

Take a Hike! 94

- ★ In the red boxes (second aorists), there is a stem change and no σα. Instead, the ending is ον.

- ★ In the green boxes (contract verbs), the contract vowel lengthens before the σα.

- ★ The yellow boxes are aorist middle deponent. They are middle in form but active in meaning. They tend to end in ομην or αμην.

The Perfect Active Tense Stem

- ★ Look for the κα. This is very easy to see in the white and green boxes.

- ★ In the red boxes (second perfects), there is no κ, only an α. That is all there is to a second perfect. It means the kappa has dropped.

- ★ Study the different ways that the verbs are reduplicated.

- ★ In the green boxes (contract verbs), notice that the contract vowel lengthens before the κα.

- ★ The yellow boxes are aorist middle deponent. They are middle in form but active in meaning. They tend to end in ομην or αμην.

The Perfect Middle/Passive Tense Stem

- ★ Study the different ways that the verbs are reduplicated.

- ★ Notice that every one of them ends in μαι and that there is no connecting vowel.

The Aorist Passive Tense Stem

- ★ Look for the beautiful θη in every verb except for the second aorist passives.

- ★ Notice that the second aorist passives (red boxes) have no θ, just an η. That's all there is to a second aorist passive.

- ★ Notice the augments.

- ★ In the green boxes (contract verbs), notice that the contract vowel lengthens before the θη.

- ★ The two yellow boxes are odd. They are aorist passive deponents. This means that even though they are passive in form, they are active in meaning.

30. μι verbs, εἰμί

See if you can list the four twists of the μι verb from memory. (Consult the grammar if you have to.)

1.

2.

3.

4.

Translate the following sentences (which contain various forms of τίθημι).

1. τὴν ψυχήν μου τίθημι[1] ὑπὲρ τῶν προβάτων.
                                                                                             sheep.

2. Ποῦ τεθείκατε αὐτόν;
     Where

---

[1] Here in the sense of "lay down."

3. οἱ μαθηταὶ αὐτοῦ ἦλθον[1] καὶ ἦραν[2] τὸ πτῶμα
   corpse
   αὐτοῦ καὶ ἔθηκαν αὐτὸ ἐν μνημείῳ.
   tomb

4. θήσω τὸ πνεῦμά μου ἐπ' αὐτόν.

---

[1] ἔρχομαι, a deponent with a second aorist, remember?

[2] from αἴρω, a liquid aorist, remember?

εἰμί

It is impossible to overemphasize the importance of this irregular but <u>very common</u> verb. In this lesson, rather than memorizing vocabulary, work on becoming familiar with εἰμί.

Try your hand at filling out the chart from memory. Try it over and over. Believe me, you will see this word A LOT.

	Present	Imperfect	Future
	εἰμί (I am)		
1s	I am	I was	I will be
2s	you are	you were	you will be
3s	he/she/it is	he/she/it was	he/she/it will be
1p	we are	we were	we will be
2p	you (all) are	you (all) were	you (all) will be
3p	they are	they were	they will be

Moody Outlook

31. Subjunctive Mood

To "parse" a word in Greek means to provide all of its grammatical information. To parse a verb, then, means to give its tense, voice, mood, person and number.

Using the Subjunctive Mood box from the Master Chart, parse the following Greek subjunctives. I have done the first one as an example.

Remember: You can find the person and number and usually the voice by the personal endings. The tense will be either aorist or present.
- Present tense verbs will exhibit no changes from the lexical form.
- Aorist tense verbs will either have a σ (first aorist) or a stem change (second aorist). They will not be augmented because the augment indicates past time and outside of the indicative mood, tense has nothing to do with time.

Verb	Tense	Voice	Mood	Person	Number
βαπτίζωμεν	Pres	Act	Sub	1st	Pl
περιπατήσητε					
σώσῃς					
προσελθώμεθα					
ποιηθῇ					

Subjunctive Mood

★ **Present** and **Aorist** tenses only
★ Look for lengthened connecting vowel
★ Look for a subjunctive when you see:

ἵνα (in order that)
ὅταν (whenever)
ὅς ἄν (whoever)
ὅπου ἄν (wherever)
ἕως (until) ἕως ἄν (until)
ἐάν (if)

	Present		Aorist		
	Active	M/P	active	middle	passive
	λύω	λύωμαι	λύσω	λύσωμαι	λυθῶ
	λύῃς	λύῃ	λύσῃς	λύσῃ	λυθῇς
	λύῃ	λύηται	λύσῃ	λύσηται	λυθῇ
	λύωμεν	λυώμεθα	λύσωμεν	λυσώμεθα	λυθῶμεν
	λύητε	λύησθε	λύσητε	λύσησθε	λυθῆτε
	λύωσιν	λύωνται	λύσωσιν	λύσωνται	λυθῶσιν
	"that I might..."	"that I might be..."	"that I might..."	"that I might... (for myself)"	"that I might be..."

Take a Hike! 100

Translate the following sentences.

1. Ἐὰν ἀγαπᾶτέ με, τὰς ἐντολὰς τὰς ἐμὰς τηρήσετε.

2. οὐ γὰρ ἀπέστειλεν ὁ θεὸς τὸν υἱὸν εἰς τὸν κόσμον ἵνα κρίνῃ
    (ἀποστέλλω)

   τὸν κόσμον, ἀλλ' ἵνα σωθῇ ὁ κόσμος δι' αὐτοῦ.
                        (σώζω)

3. ὃς δ' ἂν πίῃ ἐκ τοῦ ὕδατος οὗ ἐγὼ δώσω αὐτῷ, οὐ μὴ διψήσει
   But whoever (might drink)   (δίδωμι)   (he will thirst)

   εἰς τὸν αἰῶνα.

4. ἀμὴν λέγω ὑμῖν, ὃς ἂν μὴ δέξηται τὴν βασιλείαν τοῦ θεοῦ ὡς
                    Whoever   (δέχομαι)

   παιδίον, οὐ μὴ εἰσέλθῃ εἰς αὐτήν.
                (εἰσέρχομαι)

5. λέγει τοῖς μαθηταῖς· Ἄγωμεν εἰς τὴν Ἰουδαίαν πάλιν.
   Judea

Please supply the correct subjunctive ending to the Greek verb to convey the English meaning.

English	Greek
that we might continue to believe (present)	πιστευ
that we might believe (aorist)	πιστευ
that you (all) might continue to believe (present)	πιστευ
that you (all) might believe (aorist)	πιστευ
That they might be continue to be taught (present)	δίδασκ
That they might be taught (aorist)	δίδασκ

32. Imperative Mood

Using the Imperative Mood box from the Master Chart, parse the following Greek imperatives. I have done the first one as an example.

Remember: You can find the person and number and usually the voice by the personal endings. The tense will be either aorist or present.

- Present tense verbs will exhibit no changes from the lexical form.
- Aorist tense verbs will either have a σ (first aorist) or a stem change (second aorist). They will not be augmented because the augment indicates past time and outside of the indicative mood, tense has nothing to do with time.

Imperative Mood

	active	middle	passive
Pr	2s λῦε (You) loose! 3s λυέτω Let him loose! 2p λύετε (You) loose! 3p λυέτωσαν Let them loose!	(You) loose (for yourself)! Let him loose (for himself)! (You) loose (for yourself)! Let them loose (for themselves)!	2s λύου (You) be loosed! 3s λυέσθω Let him be loosed! 2p λύεσθε (You) be loosed! 3p λυέσθωσαν Let them be loosed!
Ao	2s λῦσον (You) loose! 3s λυσάτω Let him loose! 2p λύσατε (You) loose! 3p λυσάτωσαν Let them loose!	2s λῦσαι 3s λυσάσθω same as above 2p λύσασθε 3p λυσάσθωσαν	2s λύθητι (You) be loosed! 3s λυθήτω Let him be loosed! 2p λύθητε (You) be loosed! 3p λυθήτωσαν Let them be loosed!
2 Ao	2nd Aorist is identical to present except for the stem change in present and middle. Drops the θ in the passive.		

Verb	Tense	Voice	Mood	Person	Number
ἄκουε	Pres	Act	Imp	2nd	Sin
θέλησον					
βλεπέτωσαν					
ὑπάγετε (assume it is imperative)					
ἐκβλήθητι					

Translate the following sentences.

1. ὃ ἠκούσατε ἀπ' ἀρχῆς, ἐν ὑμῖν μενέτω.
   What (ἀκούω)   (μένω)

2. ἐν τοῖς ἔργοις πιστεύετε. (Could be translated two ways)

3. λέγει ἡ μήτηρ αὐτοῦ τοῖς διακόνοις· Ὅ τι ἂν λέγῃ ὑμῖν
                                servants   (=whatever)

   ποιήσατε.
   (ποιέω)

4. εἶπεν αὐτῷ· Ὕπαγε νίψαι εἰς τὴν κολυμβήθραν τοῦ Σιλωάμ.
   (λέγω)   (ὑπάγω) (νίπτω = wash)   pool

5. ἐκραύγασαν λέγοντες· Σταύρωσον σταύρωσον. λέγει αὐτοῖς ὁ
   They cried out (saying) (σταυτόω = crucify)

   Πιλᾶτος· Λάβετε αὐτὸν ὑμεῖς καὶ σταυρώσατε.
            (λαμβάνω)

Take a Hike! 104

Supply the imperative endings to give a Greek translation of the English.

English	Greek
(you plural) Keep on believing! (present)	πιστευ
(you singular) Believe! (aorist)	πιστευ
Let her keep on believing! (present)	πιστευ
Let them believe! (aorist)	πιστευ
(you plural) Be taught! (aorist)	δίδασκ
Let him be taught! (aorist)	δίδασκ

33. Infinitives

Use the infinitives chart and your lexicon to translate the following sentences.

	Infinitive		
	active	middle	passive
Pr	λύειν to loose	λύεσθαι to loose (for self)	λύεσθαι to be loosed
Ao	λῦσαι to loose	λύσασθαι to loose (for self)	λυθῆναι to be loosed
2 Ao	λαβεῖν to take	λαμβανω (I take)	λαβέσθαι to take (for self)
Pf	λελυκέναι to have loosed	to have loosed (for self)	λελύσθαι to have been loosed

1. δύναται εἰς τὴν κοιλίαν τῆς μητρὸς αὐτοῦ
                                  womb

   δεύτερον εἰσελθεῖν καὶ γεννηθῆναι;
   again   (ἔρχομαι)   (γεννάω)

2. Ἐγὼ βρῶσιν ἔχω φαγεῖν ἣν ὑμεῖς οὐκ οἴδατε.
         food   (ἐσθίω)

Take a Hike! 106

3. πῶς δύνασθε πιστεῦσαι;[1]

4. πολλὰ ἔχω ὑμῖν λέγειν, ἀλλ' οὐ δύνασθε
(πολύς)
βαστάζειν[2] αὐτό.

5. ὀφείλομεν[3] ἀλλήλους ἀγαπᾶν[4].

---

[1] Don't forget to look at the punctuation!

[2] βαστάζω = I bear

[3] ὀφείλω = I ought

[4] Remember that this is a contract verb (ἀγαπάω). The ending is slightly hidden by the contraction.

6. οὐδεὶς ἄξιος εὑρέθη ἀνοῖξαι[1] τὸ βιβλίον οὔτε
   worthy   (εὑρίσκω) (ἀνοίγω)   book

βλέπειν αὐτό.

7. ἔπεσον[2] ἔμπροσθεν τῶν ποδῶν αὐτοῦ
             before   (πούς)

προσκυνῆσαι

(Challenge question. All the words are in your vocabulary list. I'll give no clues except to tell you that this is one of the idiomatic uses of the infinitive.)

8. τῆς ἀληθείας οὐκ ἐδέξαντο εἰς τὸ σωθῆναι

αὐτούς.

---

[1] The ending is slightly hidden by the collision of consonants.

[2] πίπτω = I fall

Participle Panorama

34. Participles Overview

What is a participle?

As verbals, Greek participles have... (check all that apply)
- ☐ Tense
- ☐ Voice
- ☐ Mood
- ☐ Person
- ☐ Number

As adjectives, participles have... (check all that apply)
- ☐ Case
- ☐ Number
- ☐ Gender

How many forms of each participle are there?
- ☐ 1
- ☐ 24

As adjectives, participles follow the _____ and _____ patterns of declension.
- ☐ 2-2 and 2-2
- ☐ 2-1-2 and 3-3
- ☐ 2-1-2 and 3-1-3

In the following sentences, please do two things:
   a. Identify whether the participle is being used adjectivally, substantivally, or adverbially.
   b. Underline the participial phrase.

1. Cooking with my wife is my favorite thing to do after a long day at the office.
   - ☐ Adjectival
   - ☐ Substantival
   - ☐ Adverbial

2. I went to sleep after reading the entire newspaper.
   - ☐ Adjectival
   - ☐ Substantival
   - ☐ Adverbial

3. The Running Man is not a very good movie.
    - ☐ Adjectival
    - ☐ Substantival
    - ☐ Adverbial

4. She fell out of her chair after falling asleep in class.
    - ☐ Adjectival
    - ☐ Substantival
    - ☐ Adverbial

5. The Jumping Frogs of Calaveras County is one of Mark Twain's most famous books.
    - ☐ Adjectival
    - ☐ Substantival
    - ☐ Adverbial

6. Jumping is what frogs do.
    - ☐ Adjectival
    - ☐ Substantival
    - ☐ Adverbial

7. After watching the movie, they went out for dessert.
    - ☐ Adjectival
    - ☐ Substantival
    - ☐ Adverbial

35. Present Participles

The only way to get used to participles is to dive in. So here we go! In each sentence, please
- ✓ parse the participle
- ✓ determine whether it is adjectival, substantival, or adverbial
- ✓ underline the participial phrase (if there is one)
- ✓ provide a translation.

1. ὁ πιστεύων[1] εἰς τὸν υἱὸν ἔχει ζωὴν αἰώνιον
                           son   (ἔχω)

2. Μεσσίας ἔρχεται, ὁ λεγόμενος χριστός.
                        (λέγω)

3. λέγει αὐτῇ ὁ Ἰησοῦς· Ἐγώ εἰμι, ὁ λαλῶν σοι.
                                      (λαλέω)

---

[1] I'm giving this one away, but I need to tell you that with substantival participles like this you are free to provide the implied subject. In this case, you may translate ὁ πιστεύων as "He who believes." Literally it is closer to "the believing one."

Take a Hike! 112

4. ἠρώτων αὐτὸν οἱ μαθηταὶ λέγοντες· Ῥαββί,
   (they) were begging   (λέγω)

   φάγε[1].
   (ἐσθίω)

5. πᾶς ὁ ζῶν καὶ πιστεύων εἰς ἐμὲ οὐ μὴ
      (ζάω)   (πιστεύω)

   ἀποθάνῃ[2] εἰς τὸν αἰῶνα
   (ἀποθνήσκω)   = forever!

6. τρεῖς εἰσιν οἱ μαρτυροῦντες, τὸ πνεῦμα καὶ
                  (μαρτυρέω)

   τὸ ὕδωρ καὶ τὸ αἷμα

---

[1] Remember your second person imperative endings? This is a second aorist imperative, second person singular.

[2] Remember this construction? οὐ μή plus the aorist subjunctive is the most emphatic way to negate something in Greek.

Take a Hike! 113

7. ταῦτα τὰ ῥήματα ἐλάλησεν ἐν τῷ
   = these words   (λαλέω)

   γαζοφυλακίῳ διδάσκων ἐν τῷ ἱερῷ
   treasury   (διδάσκω)   (ἱερόν)

(Challenge sentence! I only gave you the one word we have not seen. The rest you can look up.)

8. ἐλάλησεν ὁ Ἰησοῦς λέγων· Ἐγώ εἰμι τὸ φῶς

   τοῦ κόσμου· ὁ ἀκολουθῶν ἐμοὶ οὐ μὴ

   περιπατήσῃ ἐν τῇ σκοτίᾳ, ἀλλ' ἕξει τὸ φῶς
                         darkness

   τῆς ζωῆς.

36. Aorist Participles

In each sentence, please
- ✓ parse the participle
- ✓ determine whether it is adjectival, substantival, or adverbial
- ✓ underline the participial phrase (if there is one)
- ✓ provide a translation.

1. οὐ ζητῶ τὸ θέλημα τὸ ἐμὸν ἀλλὰ τὸ θέλημα τοῦ πέμψαντός με.
   (ζητέω)   my   (πέμπω)

2. Οὗτός ἐστιν ὁ μαθητὴς ὁ γράψας ταῦτα.
   (εἰμί)   (γράφω)

3. ἔφαγον τὸν ἄρτον εὐχαριστήσαντος τῷ κυρίῳ.
   (ἐσθίω)   (εὐχαριστέω = I give thanks)

Take a Hike! 115

4. Ἐγώ εἰμι ὁ ἄρτος ὁ καταβὰς ἐκ τοῦ οὐρανοῦ.
   (καταβαίνω)

5. ταῦτα εἰπὼν ἔμεινεν ἐν τῇ Γαλιλαίᾳ.
   These things   (μένω)   (sound it out)

6. ἦλθεν Νικόδημος, ὁ ἐλθὼν πρὸς αὐτὸν
   (ἔρχομαι)   (sound it out)   (ἔρχομαι)

   νυκτός.
   = by night.

7. μακάριοι οἱ μὴ ἰδόντες καὶ πιστεύσαντες.
   (ὁράω)

8. αὕτη ἐστὶν ἡ νίκη ἡ νικήσασα τὸν κόσμον, ἡ
   (οὗτος)   victory   (νικάω = I conquer)

   πίστις ἡμῶν·

37. Perfect Participles

In each sentence, please
- ✓ parse the participle
- ✓ determine whether it is adjectival, substantival, or adverbial
- ✓ underline the participial phrase (if there is one)
- ✓ provide a translation.

1. τὸ γεγεννημένον ἐκ τῆς σαρκὸς σάρξ ἐστιν.
   (γεννάω)   (εἰμί)

2. ἔλεγον μετ' ἀλλήλων ἐν τῷ ἱερῷ ἑστηκότες.[1]
   (λέγω = they were talking)   (ἵστημι)

3. Ἔλεγεν ὁ Ἰησοῦς πρὸς τοὺς πεπιστευκότας
   (λέγω)
   αὐτῷ Ἰουδαίους· Ἐὰν ὑμεῖς μείνητε ἐν τῷ
                                        (μένω)
   λόγῳ τῷ ἐμῷ, ἀληθῶς μαθηταί μού ἐστε.
          my   truly   (εἰμί)

---

[1] μι verbs can throw you. Look at the Principal parts chart for clarity. The κοτ gives it away as a perfect. The reduplication is vocalic so it is harder to see.

Take a Hike! 118

4. ὁ ἑωρακὼς[1] ἐμὲ ἑώρακεν τὸν πατέρα.
   (ὁράω)   (ὁράω)

5. αἰτεῖτε[2] καὶ λήμψεσθε,[3] ἵνα ἡ χαρὰ ὑμῶν ᾖ[4]
   (αἰτέω)   (λαμβάνω)   (εἰμί)

   πεπληρωμένη.
   (πληρόω)

---

[1] You might want to consult the Principal parts chart for this strange word.

[2] Hint: This is an imperative.

[3] The Principal parts chart will help you here. This is a future deponent that has an odd form.

[4] Subjunctive form of εἰμί. See εἰμί in the Master Chart, page 6.

Take a Hike! 119

6. ἐγὼ ἐν αὐτοῖς καὶ σὺ ἐν ἐμοί, ἵνα ὦσιν[1]
(εἰμί)

τετελειωμένοι εἰς ἕν.[2]
(τελειόω = I complete)

(this one is tricky because of the word order)
7. ὁ ἑωρακὼς[3] μεμαρτύρηκεν, καὶ ἀληθινὴ
(ὁράω)   (μαρτυρέω)   true

αὐτοῦ ἐστιν ἡ μαρτυρία.
      (εἰμί)   witness

---

[1] Are you beginning to see how important it is to get used to the various forms of εἰμί? They are all over the place. This is a subjunctive form (Master Chart page 6). It means "they might be."

[2] Don't miss the rough breathing. Εἷς, μία, ἕν, remember? Look up εἷς if not.

[3] Here it is again! Look at ὁράω in the Principal parts chart. Notice the perfect form.

ANSWERS

GREEK
FOR EVERYONE

Base Camp

Know your ABC's

GREEK FOR EVERYONE

1. Grammar Overview

Check Your Understanding

In the following paragraph:
- Circle the nouns.
- Underline the articles.
- Put a box around the adjectives.
- Cross out the pronouns.

<u>The</u> [biggest] (obstacle) to learning (Greek) is (fear.)
~~It~~ causes [weak] (people) to give up.
[Valiant] (students) fight through (fear) until ~~they~~ conquer ~~it~~!

In the following paragraph:
- Circle the verbs.
- Underline the adverbs.
- Put a box around the participles.
- Cross out the infinitives.

<u>Very</u> few people (like) ~~to exercise~~.
Even though activities like [running] and [jogging] (can be) enjoyable,
almost no one (does) these things <u>happily</u>.

In the following paragraph:
- Circle the conjunctions.
- Underline the prepositions.

Julie (and) I love Northern California
(but) the heat sometimes drives us <u>up</u> the wall.
We do not plan to move (because) we are comfortable <u>in</u> our house.

3. Vowels, Diphthongs, Syllables, Punctuation

2. What is a diphthong?

Two vowels that make a single sound.

6. Underline the vowels or diphthongs in the following words. Next, divide the words into syllables by placing slash marks between them.

   Remember: One syllable per vowel or diphthong.

κύ-ρι-ος (Lord)	πνεῦ-μα (Spirit)
μα-θη-τής (disciple)	ἄγ-γε-λος (angel)
ἡ-μέ-ρα (day)	ἁ-μαρ-τί-α (sin)
εἰ (if)	βα-σι-λεί-α (kingdom)
με-τά (with)	δό-ξα (glory)
οὖν (therefore)	ἔθ-νος (nation)
πα-τήρ (father)	ἔρ-γον (deed)
πίσ-τις (faith)	καρ-δί-α (heart)
πισ-τεύ-ω (I believe)	κόσ-μος (universe)

4. Pronunciation, Accents, Breathing Marks

Syllabification of John 1:1-14

1 Ἐν ἀρ-χῇ ἦν ὁ λό-γος, καὶ ὁ λό-γος ἦν πρὸς τὸν θε-όν, καὶ θε-ὸς ἦν ὁ λό-γος.

2 οὗ-τος ἦν ἐν ἀρ-χῇ πρὸς τὸν θε-όν.

3 πάν-τα δι' αὐ-τοῦ ἐ-γέ-νε-το, καὶ χω-ρὶς αὐ-τοῦ ἐ-γέ-νε-το οὐ-δὲ ἕν.

ὃ γέ-γο-νεν 4 ἐν αὐ-τῷ ζω-ὴ ἦν, καὶ ἡ ζω-ὴ ἦν τὸ φῶς τῶν ἀν-θρώ-πων·

5 καὶ τὸ φῶς ἐν τῇ σκο-τί-ᾳ φαί-νει, καὶ ἡ σκο-τί-α αὐ-τὸ οὐ κα-τέ-λα-βεν.

6 Ἐ-γέ-νε-το ἄν-θρω-πος, ἀ-πε-σταλ-μέ-νος πα-ρὰ θε-οῦ, ὄ-νο-μα αὐ-τῷ Ἰ-ω-άν-νης·

7 οὗ-τος ἦλ-θεν εἰς μαρ-τυ-ρί-αν ἵ-να μαρ-τυ-ρή-σῃ πε-ρὶ τοῦ φω-τός, ἵ-να πάν-τες πι-στεύ-σω-σιν δι' αὐ-τοῦ.

8 οὐκ ἦν ἐ-κεῖ-νος τὸ φῶς, ἀλλ' ἵ-να μαρ-τυ-ρή-σῃ πε-ρὶ τοῦ φω-τός.

9 Ἦν τὸ φῶς τὸ ἀ-λη-θι-νόν, ὃ φω-τί-ζει πάν-τα ἄν-θρω-πον, ἐρ-χό-με-νον εἰς τὸν κόσ-μον.

10 ἐν τῷ κόσ-μῳ ἦν, καὶ ὁ κόσ-μος δι' αὐ-τοῦ ἐ-γέ-νε-το, καὶ ὁ κόσ-μος αὐ-τὸν οὐκ ἔ-γνω.

11 εἰς τὰ ἴ-δι-α ἦλ-θεν, καὶ οἱ ἴ-δι-οι αὐ-τὸν οὐ παρ-έ-λα-βον.

12 ὅ-σοι δὲ ἔ-λα-βον αὐ-τόν, ἔ-δω-κεν αὐ-τοῖς ἐξ-ου-σί-αν τέκ-να θε-οῦ γε-νέσ-θαι, τοῖς πι-στεύ-ου-σιν εἰς τὸ ὄ-νο-μα αὐ-τοῦ,

13 οἳ οὐκ ἐξ αἱ-μά-των οὐ-δὲ ἐκ θε-λή-μα-τος σαρ-κὸς οὐ-δὲ ἐκ θε-λή-μα-τος ἀν-δρὸς ἀλλ' ἐκ θε-οῦ ἐ-γεν-νή-θη-σαν.

14 Καὶ ὁ λό-γος σὰρξ ἐ-γέ-νε-το καὶ ἐ-σκή-νω-σεν ἐν ἡ-μῖν, καὶ ἐ-θε-α-σά-μεθα τὴν δό-ξαν αὐ-τοῦ, δό-ξαν ὡς μο-νο-γεν-οῦς παρὰ πα-τρός, πλή-ρης χά-ρι-τος καὶ ἀ-λη-θεί-ας.

The Crossroads
Conjunctions and Prepositions

GREEK FOR EVERYONE

5. Conjunctions

- It is raining tonight <u>but</u> I expect it to stop soon.

- <u>If</u> you keep up this pace <u>then</u> you will soon read Greek like Aristotle did!

- I study Greek <u>in order to</u> develop my vocabulary.

- I am not a fan of country music, <u>nevertheless</u>, I enjoy the concerts.

- Classical musicians do not play the violin <u>like</u> bluegrass players do.

- We have been saving money, <u>therefore</u> we will be able go to Europe.

- You will find the keys <u>where</u> I left them under the doormat.

- You will feel spectacular <u>when</u> you master Greek.

- I am hungry <u>and</u> McDonalds has a special on Big Macs <u>so</u> I am headed there to eat.

6. Prepositions

Underline the prepositions and objects in the following English sentences.

- <u>Over the river</u> and <u>through the woods,</u> <u>to grandmother's house</u> we go!

- There is nowhere I would rather be than sitting <u>beside the lake</u> with a fish <u>on the line</u>.

- I am <u>in love</u>!

- <u>In a year</u> I will be fifty years old.

- Too much partying can get you <u>into trouble</u>.

- I need a get <u>out of jail</u> free card!

- Because of the mortgage meltdown, many American families are <u>under water</u>.

Noun Rest

GREEK FOR EVERYONE

7. Nouns

Every Greek noun will be defined by three important attributes:

1. Case
2. Number
3. Gender

Fill out the chart below from memory.

Case	Number	Gender
Nominative **G**enitive **D**ative **A**ccusative	**S**ingular **P**lural	**M**asculine **F**eminine **N**euter

Match the case with its function in the sentence.

C Nominative	A	Object of the verb (receives the action)
D Genitive	B	Indirect object
B Dative	C	Subject of the verb (does the action)
A Accusative	D	Possession

True or False

T Every Greek noun is either masculine or feminine or neuter.

8. First Declension

(Phrases)

ἀγάπη ζωῆς
love of life

ἡμέρα δόξης
day of glory

(Sentences)

1. ἡ ἐκκλησία ἔχει τὴν ἐξουσίαν τῆς βασιλείας.
   The church has the authority of the kingdom.

2. ἡ καρδία τῆς ἁμαρτίας μισεῖ ἀλήθειαν.
   The heart of sin hates truth.

3. ζωήν τῇ γῇ ἡ ψυχή τῆς ἀγάπης συνάξει.
   The soul of love will bring life to the earth.

4. ἡ ἐκκλησία ἐμαρτύρησεν τῇ δοξῇ τῆς ὥρας.
   The church bore witness to the glory of the hour.

5. ψύχας ἁμαρτίαι λύουσιν.
   Sins destroy souls.

6. ἀγαπήσεις τὴν βασιλείαν τῇ καρδίᾳ.
   You must love the Kingdom with the heart. (or "in the heart")

7. ἀλήθεια δίδωσιν δόχαν τῇ ψυχῇ.
   Truth gives glory to the soul.

8. ἡ ἐκκλησία κηρύσσει ζωήν τῇ γῇ.
   The church preaches life to the earth.

9. ἡ ψυχή γνώσεται τὴν ἡμέραν καὶ τὴν ὥραν.
   The soul will know the day and the hour

10. φωνή επρχεται τῇ γῇ
    Sound goes out to the earth.

9. Second Declension

1. θεός ἀγάπᾳ τὸν κόσμον.
   God loves the world.

2. τὸν κόσμον θεός ἀγάπᾳ.
   God loves the world.

3. ὁ κόσμος θεόν ἀγάπᾳ.
   The world loves God.

4. ὁ κύριος ἐκήρυξεν τὸ εὐαγγέλιον ἀνθρώποις.
   The Lord preached the gospel   to men

5. ἐκήρυξεν ὁ κύριος ἀνθρώποις τὸ εὐαγγέλιον τοῦ θεοῦ.
   The Lord preached the gospel of God to men

6. τοὺς ἀγγέλους τοῦ οὐρανοῦ ὁ κύριος ἀγάπᾳ.
   The Lord loves the angels of heaven.

7. τεκνία ἐν οὐρανῷ ὄψονται τὸν πρόσωπον τοῦ θεοῦ.
   Children in heaven will see the Face of God.

8. Τοῖς τεκνία τῶν ἀνθρώπων ἐδόθη ὁ νόμος τοῦ κυρίου.
   The law of the Lord was given to the children of men.

9. Τό πρόσωπον ἀδελφοῦ φέρει δόξαν τῷ κόσμῳ.
   The face of a brother brings glory to the world.

10. ἄγγελοι κυκλεύουσιν τό ἱερόν.
    Angels surround the temple.

11. ὁ θεὸς τοῦ οὐρανοῦ πέμπει ἄγγελοι τῷ κόσμῳ.
    The God of heaven sends angels to the world.

12. Ἄγγελοι ποιοῦσιν τὸ ἔργον τοῦ θεοῦ ἐν τῷ ἱερῷ.
    Angels do the work of God in the temple.

10. Third Declension

1. χάρις ἔσωσεν τὸν πατέρα.
Grace saved the father.

2. πίστις σῴζει ἄνδρας καὶ γυναῖκας τῇ δυνάμει τῆς χάριτος.
Faith saves men and women by the power of grace.

3. ὁ βασιλεύς βασιλεύει τὸν πόλιν ἐν δυνάμει.
The king rules the city in power.

4. ἡ πόλις πληροῖ τῷ αἷμα τῶν πατέρων.
The city is filled with the blood of the fathers.

5. τὸ πνεῦμα νικᾷ χάριτι.
The Spirit conquers by grace.

6. ὁ πατήρ ἐνέκρυψεν τὸ ὄνομα τῆς γυναικός.
The father concealed the name of the woman.

7. ὁ βασιλεύς ἔχει αἷμα ἐπὶ τάς χείρας αὐτοῦ.
The King has blood on his hands.

8. αἷμα δίδωσιν δύναμιν τῷ σώματι.
Blood gives power to the body.

9. ἡ πόλις πληροῖ τῷ αἷματι τῶν ἀρχιερέων.
The city is filled with the blood of the chief priests.

10. χάρις οὐ ἔρχεται τῇ χειρὶ ἀνδρῶν.
Grace does not come by the hand of men.

Camp Modifier

The Article and Adjectives

GREEK FOR EVERYONE

11. The Article

Questions

<u>a</u> Articles must match the noun they modify in:
    a. Case, Number and Gender
    b. Declension
    c. Case and Number
    d. Number and Gender

<u>b</u> Why are there twenty four forms of the article but only eight forms of every noun?
    a. Because articles are made of only a few letters.
    b. Because articles have to be able to be masculine <u>and</u> feminine <u>and</u> neuter.
    c. Because articles have more than four cases.
    d. There is no logical explanation.

Match the article with the noun it modifies.

5	τοῖς	1	λόγους
3	τῆς	2	τέκνον
1	τούς	3	ἡμερῆς
4	τῶν	4	πίστεων
2	τό	5	ἀδελφοῖς

12. 2-1-2 Adjectives

	Adjective (ἅγιος, ἁγία, ἅγιον)	Noun	Translation
1	ἁγίᾳ	ζωῇ	to a holy life
2	ἁγίους	λόγους	holy words
3	ἁγίων	λογῶν	of holy words
4	ἁγίαις	ζωαῖς	to holy lives
5	ἅγια	ἔργα	holy works
6	ἅγιαι	δόξαι	holy glories
7	ἁγία	καρδία	a holy heart
8	ἁγίοις	ἀγγέλοις	to holy angels
9	ἁγίου	ἐργοῦ	of a holy work
10	ἁγίαν	ἐκκλησίαν	a holy church
	The ones below are trickier since they are third declension nouns. (The endings may not look the same.)		
11	ἁγίου	ἀνδρός	of a holy man
12	ἁγίῳ	ὀνόματι	to a holy name
13	ἅγιαι	χάριτες	holy graces
14	ἁγίων	βασιλέων	of holy kings
15	ἁγίαν	πίστιν	a holy faith

13. 3-1-3 Adjectives

	Adjective (πᾶς, πᾶσα, πᾶν)	Noun	Translation
1	παντί	ζωῇ	to every life
2	πάντας	λόγους	all words
3	πάντων	νομῶν	of all laws
4	πάσαις	ψυχαῖς	to all souls
5	πάντα	ἔργα	all works
6	πᾶσαι	ἡμέραι	all days
7	πᾶσα	καρδία	every heart
8	πᾶσιν	ἀγγέλοις	to all angels
9	παντός	εὐαγγελίου	of every gospel
10	πᾶσαν	ἀλήθειαν	every truth

	3 masc	1 fem	3 neut
N	πας	πασα	παν
G	παντος	πασης	παντος
D	παντι	παση	παντι
A	παντα	πασαν	παν
N	παντες	πασαι	παντα
G	παντων	πασων	παντων
D	πασι[ν]	πασαις	πασι[ν]
A	παντας	πασας	παντα

	Adjective (πᾶς, πᾶσα, πᾶν)	**Noun**	**Translation**
	Note: The words below are third declension nouns		
11	παντός	ἀνδρός	of every man
12	παντί	ὀνόματι	to every name
13	πᾶσαι	χάριτες	all graces
14	πάντων	βασιλέων	of all kings
15	πᾶσαν	πίστιν	all faith

	3 masc	1 fem	3 neut
N	πας	πασα	παν
G	παντος	πασης	παντος
D	παντι	παση	παντι
A	παντα	πασαν	παν
N	παντες	πασαι	παντα
G	παντων	πασων	παντων
D	πασι[ν]	πασαις	πασι[ν]
A	παντας	πασας	παντα

14. 2-2 & 3-3 Adjectives

ἁμαρτωλός [2-2]		
	(2) Masculine and (2) Feminine	(2) Neuter
n	ἁμαρτωλος	ἁμαρτωλον
g	ἁμαρτωλου	ἁμαρτωλου
d	ἁμαρτωλῳ	ἁμαρτωλῳ
a	ἁμαρτωλον	ἁμαρτωλον
n	ἁμαρτωλοι	ἁμαρτωλα
g	ἁμαρτωλων	ἁμαρτωλων
d	ἁμαρτωλοις	ἁμαρτωλοις
a	ἁμαρτωλους	ἁμαρτωλα

μείζων [3-3]		
	(3) Masculine and (3) Feminine	(3) Neuter
n	μειζων	μειζον
g	μειζονος	μειζονος
d	μειζονι	μειζονι
a	μειζονα	μειζον
n	μειζονες	μειζονα
g	μειζονων	μειζονων
d	μειζοσι[ν]	μειζοσι[ν]
a	μειζονας	μειζονα

	Adjective (ἁμαρτωλός, μείζων)	Noun	Translation
1 sinful	ἁμαρτωλῳ	ζωῇ	to a sinful life
2 greater	μειζονας	λόγους	greater words
3 sinful	ἁμαρτωλων	νομῶν	of sinful laws
4 greater	μειζοσιν	ψυχαῖς	to greater souls
5 sinful	ἁμαρτωλα	ἔργα	sinful works
6 sinful	ἁμαρτωλοι	ἡμέραι	sinful days
7 sinful	ἁμαρτωλος	καρδία	sinful heart
8 greater	μειζοσιν	ἄγγελοις	to greater angels
9 greater	μειζονος	εὐαγγελίου	of a greater gospel
10 greater	μειζονα	ἀλήθειαν	a greater truth

ἁμαρτωλός [2-2]

	(2) Masculine and (2) Feminine	(2) Neuter
n	ἁμαρτωλός	ἁμαρτωλον
g	ἁμαρτωλου	ἁμαρτωλου
d	ἁμαρτωλῳ	ἁμαρτωλῳ
a	ἁμαρτωλον	ἁμαρτωλον
n	ἁμαρτωλοι	ἁμαρτωλα
g	ἁμαρτωλων	ἁμαρτωλων
d	ἁμαρτωλοις	ἁμαρτωλοις
a	ἁμαρτωλους	ἁμαρτωλα

μείζων [3-3]

	(3) Masculine and (3) Feminine	(3) Neuter
n	μειζων	μειζον
g	μειζονος	μειζονος
d	μειζονι	μειζονι
a	μειζονα	μειζον
n	μειζονες	μειζονα
g	μειζονων	μειζονων
d	μειζοσι[ν]	μειζοσι[ν]
a	μειζονας	μειζονα

	Adjective (ἁμαρτωλός, μείζων)	Noun	Translation
	Note: The words below are third declension nouns		
11 greater	μειζονος	ἀνδρός	of a greater man
12 sinful	ἁμαρτωλῳ	ὀνόματι	to a sinful name
13 greater	μειζονες	χάριτες	greater graces
14 sinful	ἁμαρτωλων	βασιλέων	of sinful kings
15 greater	μειζονα	πίστιν	a greater faith

15. Adjective Usage

1. 2, 3, 1

2. (below)

Greek is (difficult). When you start, you think it will be (easy), but as you go along you find out that it is (hard). Hopefully, you will have a <u>skilled</u> teacher who can guide you through the <u>murky</u> waters. Don't give up! The [persistent] will reap a <u>great</u> reward.

Jesus said that the [meek] would inherit the earth. [All] have heard this saying but [few] believe it to be (true). Instead, it seems like <u>greedy</u>, <u>immoral</u> people tend to get ahead in our <u>troubled</u> world. This is (terrible!)

3. c

Pronoun Point

Pronouns!

GREEK FOR EVERYONE

16. First and Second Person Pronouns

	Singular	Plural
First Person I We	N: I G: my D: to me A: me	N: we G: our D: to us A: us
Second Person You You	N: you G: your D: to you A: you	N: you G: your D: to you A: you

Wild Accusations

<u>My</u> mom and dad were standing beside <u>me</u> on the gravel road that ran past <u>our</u> house, happily watching <u>my</u> little sister, Jane. She was wobbling her way down a hill on a shiny pink bicycle, experiencing for the first time the wonder of unassisted balance and motion on two wheels.

Newborn skills are fragile. As the bike rolled down the hill it gained dangerous speed. Playful wobbling turned into desperate zigs and zags. Jane's path became as frantic as the look on her face. Faster and faster she went, her control diminishing as her velocity increased. A final desperate zag sent her smashing squarely into <u>me</u>. She erupted in an instinctive and outraged, "MOOOOOREEEEEE!"

<u>I</u> confess that <u>I</u> used to delight in provoking this reaction from <u>my</u> little sister. But on this occasion <u>I</u> was as innocent as the mailbox on the road beside <u>me</u>. As <u>my</u> sister

and I picked ourselves up out of the gravel, we heard mom and dad in the background, laughing uproariously at the wild ride and even wilder accusation.

I have been feeling a lot like Jane on that bike lately. As I wobble down life's road, I keep gaining speed, losing control and plowing into things. My instinct is to blame innocent bystanders.

I am slowly learning to face the facts: The only hands doing any steering are the ones attached to my own arms and if I ever want to learn to ride I must stop complaining about everyone else and take responsibility for my own collisions.

Please supply English translations for the first and second person Greek pronouns.

1st Person

Singular	Nom	ἐγώ	I
Singular	Gen	μου ἐμοῦ	my
Singular	Dat	μοι ἐμοί	to me
Singular	Acc	με ἐμέ	me
Plural	Nom	ἡμεῖς	we
Plural	Gen	ἡμῶν	our
Plural	Dat	ἡμῖν	to us
Plural	Acc	ἡμᾶς	us

2nd Person

Singular	Nom	σύ	you
Singular	Gen	σου σοῦ	your
Singular	Dat	σοι σοί	to you
Singular	Acc	σε σέ	you
Plural	Nom	ὑμεῖς	you
Plural	Gen	ὑμῶν	your
Plural	Dat	ὑμῖν	to you
Plural	Acc	ὑμᾶς	you

Match the pronoun with its definition.

6	μοι	1	your (plural)
8	σοι	2	you
1	ὑμῶν	3	us
5	ἡμῶν	4	I
2	σύ	5	our (plural)
7	ὑμῖν	6	to me
3	ἡμᾶς	7	to you (plural)
4	ἐγώ	8	to you (singular)

Underline the first and second pronouns in the following text (John 15:1-10). Do not worry that you cannot yet translate this. You will be able to soon!

15.1 Ἐγώ εἰμι ἡ ἄμπελος ἡ ἀληθινή, καὶ ὁ πατήρ μου ὁ γεωργός ἐστιν· 2 πᾶν κλῆμα ἐν ἐμοὶ μὴ φέρον καρπὸν αἴρει αὐτό, καὶ πᾶν τὸ καρπὸν φέρον καθαίρει αὐτὸ ἵνα καρπὸν πλείονα φέρῃ. 3 ἤδη ὑμεῖς καθαροί ἐστε διὰ τὸν λόγον ὃν λελάληκα ὑμῖν· 4 μείνατε ἐν ἐμοί, κἀγὼ¹ ἐν ὑμῖν. καθὼς τὸ κλῆμα οὐ δύναται καρπὸν φέρειν ἀφ' ἑαυτοῦ ἐὰν μὴ μένῃ ἐν τῇ ἀμπέλῳ, οὕτως οὐδὲ ὑμεῖς ἐὰν μὴ ἐν ἐμοὶ μένητε. 5 ἐγώ εἰμι ἡ ἄμπελος, ὑμεῖς τὰ κλήματα. ὁ μένων ἐν ἐμοὶ κἀγὼ ἐν αὐτῷ οὗτος φέρει καρπὸν πολύν, ὅτι χωρὶς ἐμοῦ οὐ δύνασθε ποιεῖν οὐδέν. 6 ἐὰν μή τις μένῃ ἐν ἐμοί, ἐβλήθη ἔξω ὡς τὸ κλῆμα καὶ ἐξηράνθη, καὶ συνάγουσιν αὐτὰ καὶ εἰς τὸ πῦρ βάλλουσιν καὶ καίεται. 7 ἐὰν μείνητε ἐν ἐμοὶ καὶ τὰ ῥήματά μου ἐν ὑμῖν μείνῃ, ὃ ἐὰν θέλητε αἰτήσασθε καὶ γενήσεται ὑμῖν· 8 ἐν τούτῳ ἐδοξάσθη ὁ πατήρ μου ἵνα καρπὸν πολὺν φέρητε καὶ γένησθε ἐμοὶ μαθηταί. 9 καθὼς ἠγάπησέν με ὁ πατήρ, κἀγὼ ὑμᾶς ἠγάπησα, μείνατε ἐν τῇ ἀγάπῃ τῇ ἐμῇ. 10 ἐὰν τὰς ἐντολάς μου τηρήσητε, μενεῖτε ἐν τῇ ἀγάπῃ μου, καθὼς ἐγὼ τὰς ἐντολὰς τοῦ πατρός μου τετήρηκα καὶ μένω αὐτοῦ ἐν τῇ ἀγάπῃ.

---

¹ καί + ἐγώ

17. Third Person Pronouns

Complete the following table *in English*.

	Singular	Plural
Third Person He-She-It They	N: he-she-it G: his-hers-its D: to him-her-it A: him-her-it	N: they G: theirs D: to them A: them

Please underline the third person pronouns in the following essay.

The Rider

I am a sucker for a John Wayne movie. For one thing, I like a world in which good and evil are clearly identified by the color of hats and horses. But also, I like justice. When the Duke rides onto the screen, I rest assured that justice follows close behind. Good and evil will soon be repaid in exact proportion to <u>their</u> magnitude. How could I not cheer?

The first time I saw the trailer for the remake of True Grit I was offended. Why remake a masterpiece? I would have gladly joined a posse to bring the Coen brothers in and lock <u>them</u> up if I had been asked. But having watched the remake four times now, I have no choice but to declare myself a fan.

Good and evil are much more complicated in the new version. Recoil from the shot that brings justice to <u>her</u> father's murderer sends Maddie sprawling into a pit. In that blackness, serpents slither from the heart of a dead man and latch onto <u>her</u> hand.

Maddie winds up a spinster, walking around with a scowl and half an arm missing. Justice is messy business.

Good and evil are not hard to tell apart; they are just hard to take apart. Our world and our souls are fields of wheat sown with tares. It is hard to distinguish the good from the bad by their surface appearance, and hidden roots are hopelessly tangled. Our shameful treatment of a truly good man who rode into town on a donkey should give us pause to question our wisdom as judges.

In Saint John's vision of the apocalypse, the same rider will appear again on the human scene, this time not on a donkey but on a white horse with the sword of justice drawn. I cannot help but cheer for justice. But if John has it right and I must one day face that rider, I know without question that cry of my heart will not be for justice but for mercy.

Please supply the English translations for the Greek third person pronoun.

		M (2)		F (1)		N (2)	
Singular	Nom	αὐτός	he	αὐτή	she	αὐτό	it
	Gen	αὐτοῦ	his	αὐτῆς	hers	αὐτοῦ	its
	Dat	αὐτῷ	to him	αὐτῇ	to her	αὐτῷ	to it
	Acc	αὐτόν	him	αὐτήν	her	αὐτό	it
Plural	Nom	αὐτοί	they	αὐταί	they	αὐτά	they
	Gen	αὐτῶν	of them	αὐτῶν	of them	αὐτῶν	of them
	Dat	αὐτοῖς	to them	αὐταῖς	to them	αὐτοῖς	to them
	Acc	αὐτούς	them	αὐτάς	them	αὐτά	them

Underline the third person pronouns in the following text. Do not worry that you cannot yet translate this. You will be able to soon!

11.1 Ἦν δέ τις ἀσθενῶν, Λάζαρος ἀπὸ Βηθανίας ἐκ τῆς κώμης Μαρίας καὶ Μάρθας τῆς ἀδελφῆς αὐτῆς. ² ἦν δὲ Μαριὰμ ἡ ἀλείψασα τὸν κύριον μύρῳ καὶ ἐκμάξασα τοὺς πόδας αὐτοῦ ταῖς θριξὶν αὐτῆς, ἧς ὁ ἀδελφὸς Λάζαρος ἠσθένει. ³ ἀπέστειλαν οὖν αἱ ἀδελφαὶ πρὸς αὐτὸν λέγουσαι· Κύριε, ἴδε ὃν φιλεῖς ἀσθενεῖ. ⁴ ἀκούσας δὲ ὁ Ἰησοῦς εἶπεν· Αὕτη[1] ἡ ἀσθένεια οὐκ ἔστιν πρὸς θάνατον ἀλλ' ὑπὲρ τῆς δόξης τοῦ θεοῦ ἵνα δοξασθῇ ὁ υἱὸς τοῦ θεοῦ δι' αὐτῆς. ⁵ ἠγάπα δὲ ὁ Ἰησοῦς τὴν Μάρθαν καὶ τὴν ἀδελφὴν αὐτῆς καὶ τὸν Λάζαρον. ⁶ ὡς οὖν ἤκουσεν ὅτι ἀσθενεῖ, τότε μὲν ἔμεινεν ἐν ᾧ ἦν τόπῳ δύο ἡμέρας·

Match the underlined English pronoun with the corresponding Greek pronoun.

5	I am sure <u>he</u> is the one.	1	αὐτόν
6	Give this candy <u>to her</u>.	2	ἡμᾶς
2	They are making life difficult for <u>us</u>.	3	αὐτοῖς
3	Give my best <u>to them</u>.	4	αὐτή
1	I find <u>him</u> a very likeable fellow.	5	αὐτός
4	<u>She</u> is my hero.	6	αὐτῇ
7	Where do you hide <u>it</u>?	7	αὐτό

[1] Note the breathing. This is not a third person pronoun.

18. Relative Pronouns

Which of the following sentences contain a relative pronoun?

- ☑ The dog <u>who lives at our house</u> is spoiled
- ☐ Whose dog is this?
- ☐ To whom do I owe the honor?
- ☑ This is the woman <u>to whom we owe the honor.</u>

		M (2)		F (1)		N (2)	
Singular	Nom	ὅς	who	ἥ	who	ὅ	which
	Gen	οὗ	of whom	ἧς	of whom	οὗ	of which
	Dat	ᾧ	to whom	ᾗ	to whom	ᾧ	to which
	Acc	ὅν	whom	ἥν	whom	ὅ	which
Plural	Nom	οἵ	who	αἵ	who	ἅ	which
	Gen	ὧν	of whom	ὧν	of whom	ὧν	of which
	Dat	οἷς	to whom	αἷς	to whom	οἷς	to which
	Acc	οὕς	whom	ἅς	whom	ἅ	which

(These do not have to be worded exactly like this.)

1. I am asking concerning whom you have given to me.
2. The star which they saw in the East led them.
3. And who does not take up the cross is not worthy of me.
4. Who has ears to hear, let him hear!
5. This is the Christ, Jesus whom I announce to you.
6. Whoever does not have, even what he has will be taken from him.
7. You have had five husbands, and whom you have is not your husband.
8. How shall they call in whom they did not believe?

ANSWERS 154 ANSWERS

19. Interrogative and Indefinite Pronouns

Which pronoun always has an accent on the first syllable?

- ☑ The interrogative pronoun
- ☐ The indefinite pronoun

Supply the Greek pronouns.

	Relative	Interrogative	Indefinite
English	who, which	who? which? what?	someone something anyone anything
Greek	ὅς, ἥ, ὅ	τίς, τί	τις, τι

Interrogative Pronoun

		M / F (3)		N (3)	
Singular	Nom	τίς	who? what?	τί	which? what?
	Gen	τίνος	of whom? of what?	τίνος	of which? of what?
	Dat	τίνι	to whom? to what?	τίνι	to which? to what?
	Acc	τίνα	whom? what?	τί	which? what?
Plural	Nom	τίνες	who? what?	τίνα	which? what?
	Gen	τίνων	of whom? of what?	τίνων	of which? of what?
	Dat	τίσιν	to whom? to what?	τίσιν	to which? to what?
	Acc	τίνας	whom? what?	τίνα	which? what?

Indefinite Pronoun

		M / F (3)		N (3)	
Singular	Nom	τις	someone something	τι	something
	Gen	τινός	of someone of something	τινός	of something
	Dat	τινί	to someone to something	τινί	to something
	Acc	τινά	someone something	τι	something
Plural	Nom	τινές	someone something	τινά	something
	Gen	τινῶν	of someone of something	τινῶν	of something
	Dat	τισίν	to someone to something	τισίν	to something
	Acc	τινάς	someone something	τινά	something

1. Who warned you to flee from the coming wrath?
2. Who gave this authority to you?
3. Who is this who speaks blasphemy?
4. Whom do you want me to release to you?
5. What do you think, Simon?
6. He had no need for <u>anyone</u> to bear witness concerning man.
7. But there are <u>some</u> of you who do not believe.
8. Is <u>anyone</u> weak among you?
9. There was <u>a certain</u> king whose son was weak.

20. Demonstrative and Reflexive Pronouns

The demonstrative pronouns follow what pattern of declension? 2-1-2

Near demonstrative pronouns are easy to recognize because they always begin with a rough breathing or a τ.

Far demonstrative pronouns always begin with ἐκειν.

Match the English pronoun with its type.

3 **this**

2 **these**

1 **that**

4 **those**

1 far demonstrative pronoun (singular)
2 near demonstrative pronoun (plural)
3 near demonstrative pronoun (singular)
4 far demonstrative pronoun (plural)

Match the Greek pronoun with its type.

4 **ἐκείνους**

2 **οὗτοι**

3 **τοῦτο**

1 **ἐκείνη**

1 far demonstrative pronoun (singular)
2 near demonstrative pronoun (plural)
3 near demonstrative pronoun (singular)
4 far demonstrative pronoun (plural)

ANSWERS 156 ANSWERS

Fill in the English translations for the near demonstrative pronoun.

		M (2)		F (1)		N (2)	
Near Demonstrative Pronoun							
Singular	Nom	οὗτος	this	αὕτη	this	τοῦτο	this
	Gen	τούτου	of this	ταύτης	of this	τούτου	of this
	Dat	τούτῳ	to this	ταύτῃ	to this	τούτῳ	to this
	Acc	τοῦτον	this	ταύτην	this	τοῦτο	this
Plural	Nom	οὗτοι	these	αὗται	these	ταῦτα	these
	Gen	τούτων	of these	τούτων	of these	τούτων	of these
	Dat	τούτοις	to these	ταύταις	to these	τούτοις	to these
	Acc	τούτους	these	ταύτας	these	ταῦτα	these

Practice filling in the endings of the far demonstrative pronoun. This is great practice for nailing the 2-1-2 pattern. See if you can do it by memory.

		M (2)		F (1)		N (2)	
Far Demonstrative Pronoun							
Singular	Nom	ἐκεῖνος	that	ἐκείνη	that	ἐκεῖνο	that
	Gen	ἐκείνου	of that	ἐκείνης	of that	ἐκείνου	of that
	Dat	ἐκείνῳ	to that	ἐκείνῃ	to that	ἐκείνῳ	to that
	Acc	ἐκεῖνον	that	ἐκείνην	that	ἐκεῖνο	that
Plural	Nom	ἐκεῖνοι	those	ἐκεῖναι	those	ἐκεῖνα	those
	Gen	ἐκείνων	of those	ἐκείνων	of those	ἐκείνων	of those
	Dat	ἐκείνοις	to those	ἐκείναις	to those	ἐκείνοις	to those
	Acc	ἐκείνους	those	ἐκείνας	those	ἐκεῖνα	those

The reflexive pronouns follow the 2-1-2 pattern of declension.

Match the first, second, and third person reflexive pronoun with the clue used to distinguish it.

2	First Person (myself, ourselves)	1	ἑ
3	Second Person (yourself, yourselves)	2	ἐμ
1	Third Person (himself, herself, itself themselves)	3	σε

Match the reflexive pronoun with its translation

5	ἐμαυτοῦ	1	themselves
3	ἑαυτῷ	2	ourselves
1	ἑαυτά	3	to himself, itself
2	ἐμαυτούς	4	to themselves
4	ἑαυταῖς	5	of myself
8	σεαυτῆς	6	yourself
7	ἑαυτῶν	7	of themselves
6	σεαυτόν	8	of yourself

1. The second is this: You shall love your neighbor as yourself.
2. You will say this parable to me: Physician, heal yourself.

Valley of the Verbs

GREEK
FOR EVERYONE

21. Tense, Voice, Mood, Person, Number

Tense	Voice	Mood	Person	Number
Present	**A**ctive	**I**ndicative	**1** First	**S**ingular
Imperfect	**M**iddle	**S**ubjunctive	**2** Second	**P**lural
Future	**P**assive	I**M**perative	**3** Third	
Aorist		(**P**articiple)*		
Pe**R**fect		(I**N**finitive)*		

Match the sentence with the correct <u>person and number</u>.

3	I love her!	1	third person plural
1	They will come later	2	third person singular
5	You (all) are making me tired.	3	first person singular
2	She will come someday.	4	first person plural
4	We will learn this yet!	5	second person plural

Match the sentence with the proper <u>voice</u>.

2	I ate the apple.	1	middle
3	I was eaten by an apple!	2	active
1	I ate an apple for myself.	3	passive

Match the sentence with the proper mood.

3	I hope we finish this one day.	1	indicative
2	Come inside!	2	imperative
1	It is getting cold outside.	3	subjunctive

Match the tense with its meaning

2	ongoing aspect, past time	1	Present
4	undefined aspect, past time	2	Imperfect
5	event in past with ongoing effects	3	Future
1	undefined or ongoing aspect, present time	4	Aorist
3	undefined aspect, future time	5	Perfect

ANSWERS 160 ANSWERS

Match the sentence with the Greek tense that best represents the action of the verb.

1	I <u>am eating</u> Ice cream.	1	Present
4	I <u>slept</u>.	2	Imperfect
5	It <u>is written</u>.	3	Future
3	I <u>will mow</u> the lawn later today.	4	Aorist
2	I <u>was being chased</u> by bees!	5	Perfect

22. Personal Endings

Match the first person singular endings with their translation

4 ω   1 I am being...
1 ομαι   2 I was...
2 ον   3 I was being...
3 ομην   4 I am...

Match the third person singular endings with their translation

3 ει   1 he/she/it was…
2 εται   2 he/she/it is being
1 ε(ν)   3 he/she/it is...
4 ετο   4 he/she/it was being...

Translate the following Greek sentences, paying close attention to the personal endings.

Primary Active Endings

1. πιστεύω τὸν θεόν.
   I believe (am believing)[1] God

2. βλέπομεν τὴν συναγωγήν.
   We see (are seeing) the synagogue.

3. διδάσκει τοὺς μαθητάς[2].
   He teaches (is teaching) the disciples.

Primary Middle/Passive
(translate as passive)

---

[1] If you are wondering about this, the primary forms in these examples are all <u>present</u> tense, which can be undefined or continuous aspect. The secondary forms are all <u>imperfect</u> tense, which can only be continuous aspect. More about this soon.

[2] Remember that this is an odd first declension masculine noun.

ANSWERS 162 ANSWERS

4. διδασκόμεθα τὴν ἀλήθειαν.
   We are taught (are being taught) the truth.

5. βλέπομαι ἐν τῇ οἰκίᾳ.
   I am seen (am being seen) in the house.

6. διδάσκῃ περὶ τοῦ εὐαγγελίου.
   You are taught (are being taught) concerning the gospel.

Secondary Active

7. ἐπίστευες τὴν ἀλήθειαν.
   You were believing the truth.

8. ἐπίστευον ἐν τῇ βασιλείᾳ.
   I was believing in the Kingdom.
   They were believing in the Kingdom.

9. ἐβλέπομεν τὴν θάλασσαν.
   We were seeing the sea.

Secondary Middle/Passive
(translate as passive)

10. Ἰησους ἐκηρύσσετο τοῖς ἔθνεσιν.
    Jesus was being preached to the nations.

11. Ἰησους ἐπέμπετο εἰς τὸν κόσμον.
    Jesus was being sent into the world.

12. τοὺς ἱεροὺς ἐλύοντο ὑπ' ἀνθρώπων.
    The temples were being destroyed by men (people).

23. Contract Verbs

5	ἀγαπῶμαι	1	We are making
7	ἀγαπᾷς	2	He is making
9	ἀγαπῶνται	3	They are making
2	ποιεῖ	4	You are filling
1	ποιοῦμεν	5	I am being loved
3	ποιοῦσι(ν)	6	You (all) are filling
4	πληροῖς	7	You are loving
10	πληροῦμαι	8	We are being filled
8	πληρούμεθα	9	They are being loved
6	πληροῦτε	10	I am being filled

24. Regular Roots & Stems

Match the clues with the proper tense.

Tense		Clues	
6	**Present** λύω	1	augment, present tense stem secondary endings
1	**Imperfect** ἔλυον	2	reduplication, κ primary active endings
8	**Future** λύσω	3	augment, σα, secondary endings
3	**Aorist** ἔλυσα	4	augment, θη secondary <u>active</u> endings
2	**Perfect Active** λέλυκα	5	θης primary m/p endings
7	**Perfect Middle/Passive** λέλυμαι	6	Present tense stem (lexical form) primary endings
4	**Aorist Passive** ἐλύθην	7	reduplication, no κ, no connecting vowel primary middle/passive endings
5	**Future Passive** λυθήσομαι	8	σ before primary endings

Match the form of πιστεύω with its translation. Remember to look for the clues.
(This is challenging. Don't despair if you find it difficult!)

3	ἐπίστευον	1	We are being believed (or we are believed)
7	πεπίστευκεν	2	You were believed
8	πιστεύσετε	3	I (or they) were believing
4	πιστευθησόμεθα	4	We will be believed
2	ἐπίστευθης	5	I believed
1	πιστεύομεθα	6	They have come to be believed
6	πεπίστευνται	7	He/She/It has come to believe
5	ἐπίστευσα	8	You (all) will believe

25. Adverbs

In the following sentences, please circle the adverb and underline the verb it modifies.

- I have to admit that I <u>prepared</u> this lesson (reluctantly).
- The problem is that adverbs <u>are</u> (not) difficult.
- Once you learn to see them you <u>identify</u> them (easily).
- I thought about <u>skipping</u> this lesson (again).
- However, I realized that some of you <u>study</u> (diligently).
- You would be annoyed (not) <u>to study</u> every part of speech.
- So I (busily) <u>prepared</u> the video, <u>wrote</u> the grammar, and <u>updated</u> the workbook.
- I hope you will (not) <u>be</u> disappointed that it is so easy!

The Labyrinth

GREEK FOR EVERYONE

26. Liquid Verbs

Greek	English	Cognates & Memory Aids
Liquid Verbs		
αἴρω	I take up, take away	An aeroplane takes you up, up, and away!
ἀναβαίνω	I go up	
ἀποκτείνω	I kill	
ἀποστέλλω	I send	Apostles are sent with a message.
βάλλω	I throw, put	Balls are thrown.
ἐγείρω	I raise up	
ἐκβάλλω	I cast out	
κρίνω	I judge, decide	Critics are often judgmental.
μέλλω	I am about to	
μένω	I remain, abide	Permanent things remain.
πίνω	I drink	Potions are drunk.
φέρω	I carry or bear	Freight is carried by trucks. Ferries are ships that carry cargo on water.
χαίρω	I rejoice	

Here are some liquid verbs in context. Underline the liquid consonant and translate the following sentences.

1. Ἐκ τοῦ στόματός σου κρίνῶ σε.

Out of your mouth, I will judge you. (= By your words I will judge you.)

2. πῶς κρινεῖ ὁ θεὸς τὸν κόσμον;

How will God judge the world?

3. ἐν δικαιοσύνῃ κρίνεῖ καὶ πολεμσεῖ.

In righteousness he will judge and make war.

4. οὐ ἔκρινά.
I did not judge.

5. ἔκρινεν τὴν πόρνην τὴν μεγάλην.
He judged the great prostitute.

6. ὁ ὄχλος ἔμεινεν.
The crowd remained.

7. κἀγὼ αὐτὸν ἀρῶ.
And I will raise him.

8. αὐτὸς ἔμεινεν ἐν τῇ Γαλιλαίᾳ.
He stayed in Galilee.

9. ἐμείναμεν ἡμέραν μίαν παρ' αὐτοῖς.
We stayed one day with them.

10. ἀποστελῶ αὐτοὺς λιμὸν καὶ θάνατον.
I will send them famine and death.

27. Second Aorists

1. ἦλθον δὲ οἱ δύο ἄγγελοι εἰς Σοδομα.
   (sound it out!)

   And the two angels came into Sodom.

2. ἦλθεν ὁ θεὸς πρὸς Βαλααμ νυκτὸς.[1]
   (sound it out!)   by night

   God came to Balaam by night.

3. ἔλαβεν κύριος ὁ θεὸς τὸν ἄνθρωπον, ὃν ἔπλασεν.
   he formed

   The Lord God took the man, whom he formed.

4. καὶ συνήγαγεν αὐτοὺς εἰς τὸν τόπον τὸν καλούμενον Ἑβραϊστὶ Ἁρμαγεδών.*
   called   in Hebrew   (sound it out!)

   And he gathered them in the place called in Hebrew, "Armageddon."

5. ὁμολογήσω αὐτοῖς ὅτι Οὐδέποτε[2] ἔγνων ὑμᾶς.
   I will say   never

   I will say to them that I never knew you.

---

[1] This is an example of how the genitive can be used to show time. "by night"

[2] This is a VERY strong way to say "never." It means "not at any time!"

6. εἶπεν δὲ πρὸς αὐτὸν ὁ ἄγγελος· Μὴ φοβοῦ, Ζαχαρία.

And the angel said to him, "Do not fear, Zechariah."

28. Deponents

1. ἔρχεται[1] εἰς τὰ ὅρια τῆς Ἰουδαίας.

    He comes to the mountains of Judea.

2. ἔρχονται εἰς χωρίον οὗ τὸ ὄνομα Γεθσημανί.
   (place) (sound it out!)

    They came to a place of which the name (is) Gethsemane.
    (= They came to a place called Gethsemane)

3. Οὐκ ἀφήσω ὑμᾶς ὀρφανούς, ἔρχομαι πρὸς ὑμᾶς.
   (I will leave) (sound it out! orphans)

    I will not leave you orphans, I am coming to you.

4. μετὰ δύο ἡμέρας τὸ πάσχα γίνεται.
   (after)

    After two days, the Passover comes.

5. δύναται ὁ θεὸς ἐκ τῶν λίθων τούτων ἐγεῖραι τέκνα τῷ Ἀβραάμ.
   (to raise up)

    God is able from these stones to raise up children to Abraham.

---

[1] This is called a "historic present." Sometimes when we are telling about something that happened in the past, we use present tense verbs to make it sound more vivid. We do it in English too. "So yesterday, I am going to the store, and a baboon jumps out from behind a bush…"

6. **Πιστεύετε ὅτι δύναμαι τοῦτο ποιῆσαι;**[1]
   to do

   Do you believe that I am able to do this?

7. **Οὐκ ἀποκρίνῃ οὐδέν;**

   Not you answer not one thing?
   = You do not answer anything?
   = You answer nothing?[2]

8. **προσευχόμεθα πάντοτε περὶ ὑμῶν.**
   always

   We pray always for you.
   = We always pray for you.

Imperfect Tense

9. **ἤρχοντο πρὸς αὐτόν.**

   They were coming to him.

---

[1] Don't forget to pay attention to punctuation!

[2] This is a good example of how in translation we often have to give up on literal translation and just say it in English.

10. πᾶς ὁ ὄχλος ἤρχετο πρὸς αὐτόν, καὶ
    all   the crowd

ἐδίδασκεν αὐτούς.
he was teaching

All the crowd was coming to him and he was teaching them.

11. ἔχοντες ἀσθενείας προσήρχοντο καὶ
    Those who were sick

ἐθεραπεύοντο.
they were being healed

Those who were sick were coming and (they) were being healed.

29. Principal Parts
Just stare and stare and stare at the chart!

30. μι verbs, εἰμί

See if you can list the four twists of the μι verb from memory. (Consult the grammar if you have to.)

1. In the present tense, μι verbs reduplicate the initial letter and separate the reduplicated consonant with an iota.

2. μι verbs use slightly different endings in the present active indicative.

3. The stem vowel of the μι verbs changes a lot. It can shorten, lengthen, or drop out completely.

4. Most of the μι verbs use κα instead of σα to indicate aorist tense. These are called "kappa aorists."

Translate the following sentences (which contain various forms of τίθημι).

1. τὴν ψυχήν μου τίθημι ὑπὲρ τῶν προβάτων.
   sheep.

   = I lay down my soul for the sheep.

2. Ποῦ τεθείκατε αὐτόν;
   Where

   Where have you laid him?

3. οἱ μαθηταὶ αὐτοῦ ἦλθον καὶ ἦραν τὸ πτῶμα
   corpse

   αὐτοῦ καὶ ἔθηκαν αὐτὸ ἐν μνημείῳ.
   tomb

   His disciples came and took his corpse and laid it in a tomb.

4. θήσω τὸ πνεῦμά μου ἐπ᾽ αὐτόν.

   I will place my Spirit on him.

Vocabulary
εἰμί

	Present	Imperfect	Future
1s	εἰμί I am	ἤμην I was	ἔσομαι I will be
2s	εἶ you are	ἦς you were	ἔσῃ you will be
3s	ἐστίν he/she/it is	ἦν he/she/it was	ἔσται he/she/it will be
1p	ἐσμέν we are	ἦμεν we were	ἐσόμεθα we will be
2p	ἐστέ you (all) are	ἦτε you (all) were	ἔσεσθε you (all) will be
3p	εἰσίν they are	ἦσαν they were	ἔσονται they will be

Moody Outlook

31. Subjunctive Mood

Verb	Tense	Voice	Mood	Person	Number
βαπτίζωμεν	Pres	Act	Sub	1st	Pl
περιπατήσητε	Aor	Act	Sub	2nd	Pl
σώσῃς	Aor	Act	Sub	2nd	Sin
προσελθώμεθα	(2) Aor	Mid	Sub	1st	Plu
ποιηθῇ	Aor	Pass	Sub	3rd	Sin

Translate the following sentences.

1. Ἐὰν ἀγαπᾶτέ με, τὰς ἐντολὰς τὰς ἐμὰς τηρήσετε.
   If you love me you will keep my commandments.

2. οὐ γὰρ ἀπέστειλεν ὁ θεὸς τὸν υἱὸν εἰς τὸν κόσμον ἵνα κρίνῃ
   (ἀποστέλλω)
   τὸν κόσμον, ἀλλ' ἵνα σωθῇ ὁ κόσμος δι' αὐτοῦ.
   (σῴζω)
   For God did not send the Son into the world in order that he might judge the world, but in order that the world might be saved through him.

3. ὃς δ' ἂν πίῃ ἐκ τοῦ ὕδατος οὗ ἐγὼ δώσω αὐτῷ, οὐ μὴ διψήσει
   But whoever (might drink)   (δίδωμι)   (he will thirst)
   εἰς τὸν αἰῶνα.
   But whoever drinks of the water which I will give to him, will absolutely never thirst--forever! (tough to translate εις τον αἰωνα!)

4. ἀμὴν λέγω ὑμῖν, ὃς ἂν μὴ δέξηται τὴν βασιλείαν τοῦ θεοῦ ὡς
                        Whoever   (δέχομαι)
   παιδίον, οὐ μὴ εἰσέλθῃ εἰς αὐτήν.
              (εἰσέρχομαι)
   Truly I am saying to you, whoever does not receive the Kingdom of God as a child, will absolutely never enter into it.

5. λέγει τοῖς μαθηταῖς· Ἄγωμεν εἰς τὴν Ἰουδαίαν πάλιν.
   Judea

He says to the disciples, "Let us go into Judea again."

Please supply the correct subjunctive ending to the Greek verb to convey the English meaning.

English	Greek
that we might continue to believe (present)	πιστευωμεν
that we might believe (aorist)	πιστευσωμεν
that you (all) might continue to believe (present)	πιστευητε
that you (all) might believe (aorist)	πιστευσητε
That they might continue to be taught (present)	δίδασκωνται
That they might be taught (aorist)	δίδαχθωσιν (διδασκθωσιν: apply the square of stops. The sigma drops. Don't worry. If you answered διδασκθην you are on the right track.)

ANSWERS **179** ANSWERS

32. Imperative Mood

Verb	Tense	Voice	Mood	Person	Number
ἄκουε	Pres	Act	Imp	2nd	Sin
θέλησον	Aor	Act	Imp	2nd	Sin
βλεπέτωσαν	Pres	Act	Imp	3rd	Pl
ὑπάγετε (assume it is imperative)	Pres	Act	Imp	2nd	Sin
ἐκβλήθητι	Aor	Pass	Ind	2nd	Sin

Translate the following sentences.

1. ὃ ἠκούσατε ἀπ' ἀρχῆς, ἐν ὑμῖν μενέτω.
   What (ἀκούω)   (μένω)
   What you heard from the beginning, let it remain in you.
   = Let what you heard from the beginning remain in you.

2. ἐν τοῖς ἔργοις πιστεύετε. (Could be translated two ways)
   Believe in the works. (imperative)
   You believe in the works. (indicative)

3. λέγει ἡ μήτηρ αὐτοῦ τοῖς διακόνοις· Ὅ τι ἂν λέγῃ ὑμῖν
                                 servants   (=whatever)
   ποιήσατε.
   (ποιέω)
   His mother says to the servants, "Whatever he says to you, do it."

4. εἶπεν αὐτῷ· Ὕπαγε νίψαι εἰς τὴν κολυμβήθραν τοῦ Σιλωάμ.
   (λέγω)   (ὑπάγω) (νίπτω = wash)   pool
   He said to him, "Go. Wash in the pool of Siloam."

5. ἐκραύγασαν λέγοντες· Σταύρωσον σταύρωσον. λέγει αὐτοῖς ὁ
   They cried out   (saying)   (στυυτόω = crucify)

Πιλᾶτος· Λάβετε αὐτὸν ὑμεῖς καὶ σταυρώσατε.
              (λάμβανω)

They cried out, saying, "Crucify! Crucify!." Pilate says to them, "You[1] take him and crucify (him).

English	Greek
(you plural) Keep on believing! (present)	πιστευετε
(you singular) Believe! (aorist)	πιστευον
Let her keep on believing! (present)	πιστευετω
Let them believe! (aorist)	πιστευσατωσαν
(you plural) Be taught! (aorist)	δίδαχθητε (διδασκθητε: apply square of stops and drop the sigma. Get used to these kinds of changes)
Let him be taught! (aorist)	δίδαχθητω (same as above)

[1] Notice that "you" here is emphatic. ὑμείς is not needed. It is added for stress.

33. Infinitives

Use the infinitives chart and your lexicon to translate the following sentences.

	Infinitive		
	active	middle	passive
Pr	λύειν to loose	λύεσθαι to loose (for self)	λύεσθαι to be loosed
Ao	λῦσαι to loose	λύσασθαι to loose (for self)	λυθῆναι to be loosed
2 Ao	λαβεῖν to take	λαμβανω (I take)	λαβέσθαι to take (for self)
Pf	λελυκέναι to have loosed	to have loosed (for self)	λελύσθαι to have been loosed

1. δύναται εἰς τὴν κοιλίαν τῆς μητρὸς αὐτοῦ
                               womb

   δεύτερον εἰσελθεῖν καὶ γεννηθῆναι;
   again   (ἔρχομαι)   (γεννάω)

   Is he able to enter into his mother's womb again and to be born?

2. Ἐγὼ βρῶσιν ἔχω φαγεῖν ἣν ὑμεῖς οὐκ οἴδατε.
       food   (ἐσθίω)

   I have food to eat which you do not know.

3. πῶς δύνασθε πιστεῦσαι;[1]

   How are you able to believe?

---

[1] Don't forget to look at the punctuation!

4. πολλὰ ἔχω ὑμῖν λέγειν, ἀλλ' οὐ δύνασθε
   (πολύς)
   βαστάζειν¹ αὐτὸ.

   I have much to say to you, but you are not able to bear it.

5. ὀφείλομεν² ἀλλήλους ἀγαπᾶν³.

   We ought to love one another.

6. οὐδεὶς ἄξιος εὑρέθη ἀνοῖξαι⁴ τὸ βιβλίον οὔτε
   worthy (εὑρίσκω) (ἀνοίγω)   book
   βλέπειν αὐτό.

   No one was found worthy to open the book neither to see it.

7. ἔπεσον⁵ ἔμπροσθεν τῶν ποδῶν αὐτοῦ
            before   (πούς)
   προσκυνῆσαι

   I (they) fell before his feet to worship.

---

¹ βαστάζω = I bear

² ὀφείλω = I ought

³ Remember that this is a contract verb (ἀγαπάω). The ending is slightly hidden by the contraction.

⁴ The ending is slightly hidden by the collision of consonants.

⁵ πίπτω = I fall

(Challenge question. All the words are in your vocab list. I'll give no clues except to tell you that this is one of the idiomatic uses of the infinitive.)

8. τῆς ἀληθείας οὐκ ἐδέξαντο εἰς τὸ σωθῆναι αὐτούς.

They did not receive the truth in order that they be saved.

Participle Panorama

34. Participles Overview

What is a participle?

A verbal adjective.

As verbs, participles have... (check all that apply)
- ☑ Tense
- ☑ Voice
- ☐ Mood
- ☐ Person
- ☐ Number

As adjectives, participles have... (check all that apply)
- ☑ Case
- ☑ Number
- ☑ Gender

How many forms of each participle are there?
- ☐ 1
- ☑ 24

As adjectives, participles follow the _____ and _____ patterns of declension.
- ☐ 2-2 and 2-2
- ☐ 2-1-2 and 3-3
- ☑ 2-1-2 and 3-1-3

In the following sentences, please do two things:

   a. Identify whether the participle is being used adjectivally, substantivally, or adverbially.

   b. Underline the participial phrase.

1. <u>Cooking with my wife</u> is my favorite thing to do after a long day at the office.
   - ☐ Adjectival
   - ☑ Substantival
   - ☐ Adverbial

2. I went to sleep <u>after reading the entire newspaper</u>.
   - ☐ Adjectival
   - ☐ Substantival
   - ☑ Adverbial

3. The <u>Running</u> Man is not a very good movie.
   - ☑ Adjectival
   - ☐ Substantival
   - ☐ Adverbial

4. She fell out of her chair <u>after falling asleep in class</u>.
   - ☐ Adjectival
   - ☐ Substantival
   - ☑ Adverbial

5. The <u>Jumping</u> Frogs of Calaveras County is on of Mark Twain's most famous books.
   - ☑ Adjectival
   - ☐ Substantival
   - ☐ Adverbial

6. <u>Jumping</u> is what frogs do.
   - ☐ Adjectival
   - ☑ Substantival
   - ☐ Adverbial

7. <u>After watching the movie</u>, they went out for dessert.
   - ☐ Adjectival
   - ☐ Substantival
   - ☑ Adverbial

35. Present Participles

1. ὁ πιστεύων[1] εἰς τὸν υἱὸν ἔχει ζωὴν αἰώνιον
   son (ἔχω)

πιστεύων

present active participle, nominative, singular, masculine.
Used substantivally

The one believing in the son has eternal life.

2. Μεσσίας ἔρχεται, ὁ λεγόμενος χριστός.
   (λέγω)

λεγόμενος

present passive participle nominative, singular, masculine.
Used adjectivally

The Messiah is coming, the one being called "Christ."

3. λέγει αὐτῇ ὁ Ἰησοῦς· Ἐγώ εἰμι, ὁ λαλῶν σοι.
   (λαλέω)

λαλῶν

present active participle, nominative, singular, masculine.
Used adjectivally

Jesus says to her, "I am! The one speaking to you."

---

[1] I'm giving this one away, but I need to tell you that with substantival participles like this you are free to provide the implied subject. In this case, you may translate ὁ πιστεύων as "He who believes." Literally it is closer to "the believing one."

4. ἠρώτων αὐτὸν οἱ μαθηταὶ λέγοντες· Ῥαββί,
   (they) were begging   (λέγω)

   φάγε¹.
   (ἐσθίω)

λέγοντες

present active participle, nominative, plural, masculine.
Used adverbially

The disciples were begging him, saying, "Rabbi, eat!"

5. πᾶς ὁ ζῶν καὶ πιστεύων εἰς ἐμὲ οὐ μὴ
        (ζάω)   (πιστεύω)

   ἀποθάνῃ² εἰς τὸν αἰῶνα
   (ἀποθνήσκω)   = forever!

ζῶν

present active participle, nominative, singular, masculine.

πιστεύων

present active participle, nominative, singular, masculine.

Both used substantivally

All (those) living and believing in me will NEVER die--forever!

---

[1] Remember your second person imperative endings? This is a second aorist imperative, second person singular.

[2] Remember this construction? οὐ μή plus the aorist subjunctive is the most emphatic way to negate something in Greek.

6. τρεῖς εἰσιν οἱ μαρτυροῦντες, τὸ πνεῦμα καὶ
(μαρτυρέω)

τὸ ὕδωρ καὶ τὸ αἷμα

μαρτυροῦντες
present active participle, nominative, plural, masculine.
Used adjectivally

There are three bearing witness, the Spirit and the water and the blood.

7. ταῦτα τὰ ῥήματα ἐλάλησεν ἐν τῷ
= these words   (λαλέω)

γαζοφυλακίῳ διδάσκων ἐν τῷ ἱερῷ
treasury   (διδάσκω)   (ἱερόν)

διδάσκων
present active participle, nominative, singular, masculine.
Used adverbially

He spoke these words in the treasury, teaching in the temple.

(Challenge sentence! I only gave you the one word we have not seen. The rest you can look up.)

8. ἐλάλησεν ὁ Ἰησοῦς λέγων· Ἐγώ εἰμι τὸ φῶς τοῦ κόσμου· ὁ ἀκολουθῶν ἐμοὶ οὐ μὴ περιπατήσῃ ἐν τῇ σκοτίᾳ, ἀλλ᾽ ἕξει τὸ φῶς τῆς ζωῆς.

darkness

λέγων
present active participle, nominative, singular, masculine.
Used adverbially

ἀκολουθῶν
present active participle, nominative, singular, masculine.
Used substantivally

Jesus spoke, saying, "I am the light of the world. The one following me will NEVER walk in the darkness, but will have the light of life."

36. Aorist Participles

1. οὐ ζητῶ τὸ θέλημα τὸ ἐμὸν ἀλλὰ τὸ θέλημα
   (ζητέω)   my
τοῦ πέμψαντός με.
    (πέμπω)

πέμψαντός
aorist, active participle, genitive, singular, masculine.
Used substantivally.

I am not seeking my will, but the will of the (one) sending me.

2. Οὗτός ἐστιν ὁ μαθητὴς ὁ γράψας ταῦτα.
         (εἰμί)   (γράφω)

γράψας
aorist, active participle, nominative, singular, masculine.
Used adjectivally.

This is the disciple writing these things.
= This is the disciple who writes these things.

3. ἔφαγον τὸν ἄρτον εὐχαριστήσαντες τῷ
   (ἐσθίω)   (εὐχαριστέω = I give thanks)
κυρίῳ.

εὐχαριστήσαντες
aorist, active, participle, genitive, masculine, singular.

They ate the bread, giving thanks to the Lord.

4. Ἐγώ εἰμι ὁ ἄρτος ὁ καταβὰς ἐκ τοῦ οὐρανοῦ.
(καταβαίνω)

καταβὰς
aorist, active participle, nominative, singular, masculine.
Used adjectivally

I am the bread coming out of heaven.

5. ταῦτα εἰπὼν ἔμεινεν ἐν τῇ Γαλιλαίᾳ.
These things   (μένω)   (sound it out)

εἰπὼν
(2nd) aorist, active, participle, nominative, singular, masculine.
Used adverbially.

Saying these things, he remained in Galilee.

6. ἦλθεν Νικόδημος, ὁ ἐλθὼν πρὸς αὐτὸν
(ἔρχομαι)   (sound it out)   (ἔρχομαι)

νυκτὸς.
= by night.

ἐλθὼν
(2nd) aorist, active, participle, nominative, singular, masculine.
Used adjectivally.

Nicodemus came, the one coming to him by night.

7. μακάριοι οἱ μὴ ἰδόντες καὶ πιστεύσαντες.
(ὁράω)

ἰδόντες
(2nd) aorist, active, participle, nominative, plural, masculine.
Used substantivally.

πιστεύσαντες
aorist, active, participle, nominative, plural, masculine.
Used substantivally.

Blessed (are) those not seeing and believing.

8. αὕτη ἐστὶν ἡ νίκη ἡ νικήσασα τὸν κόσμον, ἡ
(οὗτος)   victory   (νικάω = I conquer)

πίστις ἡμῶν·

νικήσασα
aorist, active, participle, nominative, feminine, singular.
Used adjectivally.

This is the victory conquering the world: our faith.

37. Perfect Participles

1. τὸ γεγεννημένον ἐκ τῆς σαρκὸς σάρξ ἐστιν.
(γεννάω)   (εἰμί)

γεγεννημένον
perfect, passive, participle, accusative, singular, masculine.
Used substantivally.

The one who has been born of the flesh is flesh.

2. ἔλεγον μετ' ἀλλήλων ἐν τῷ ἱερῷ ἑστηκότες.
(λέγω = they were talking)   (ἵστημι)

ἑστηκότες
perfect, active, participle, nominative, plural, masculine.
Used adverbially.

They were talking with one another, standing[1] in the temple.

---

[1] It is tough to capture the aspect of perfect participles in translation! Here, John's use of a perfect seems calculated to present the Jewish officials as a stubborn obstacle to Jesus. They don't just stand (aorist). They "stand and remain" in the temple.

3. Ἔλεγεν ὁ Ἰησοῦς πρὸς τοὺς πεπιστευκότας (λέγω) αὐτῷ Ἰουδαίους· Ἐὰν ὑμεῖς μείνητε ἐν τῷ (μένω) λόγῳ τῷ ἐμῷ, ἀληθῶς μαθηταί μού ἐστε. (εἰμί)

πεπιστευκότας
perfect, active, participle, accusative, plural, masculine
Used substantivally.

Jesus was saying to the Jews who had come to believe in Him, "If your remain in my word, truly you are my disciples."

4. ὁ ἑωρακὼς ἐμὲ ἑώρακεν τὸν πατέρα. (ὁράω) (ὁράω)

ἑωρακὼς
perfect, active, participle, nominative, singular, masculine
Used substantivally

The one who has come to see me, has come to see the father.

5. αἰτεῖτε καὶ λήμψεσθε, ἵνα ἡ χαρὰ ὑμῶν ᾖ
   (αἰτέω)   (λαμβάνω)   (εἰμί)
   πεπληρωμένη.
   (πληρόω)

πεπληρωμένη
perfect, passive, participle, nominative, singular, feminine
Used substantivally (predicate nominative).

Ask and you will receive, so that your joy may be and remain fulfilled.[1]

6. ἐγὼ ἐν αὐτοῖς καὶ σὺ ἐν ἐμοί, ἵνα ὦσιν[2]
                                              (εἰμί)
   τετελειωμένοι εἰς ἕν.
   (τελειόω = I complete)

τετελειωμένοι
perfect, passive, participle, nominative, plural, masculine
Used substantivally (predicate nominative)

I in them, and you in me, in order that they might be completed into one.[3]

---

[1] Again, the perfect is tough to capture in translation. My translation here is clumsy but accurate.

[2] Are you beginning to see how important it is to get used to the various forms of εἰμί? They are all over the place. This is a subjunctive form (Master Chart page 6). It means "they might be."

[3] Again, I am struggling to capture the idea of the perfect's aspect.

(this one is tricky because of the word order)

7. ὁ ἑωρακὼς μεμαρτύρηκεν, καὶ ἀληθινὴ
   (ὁράω)   (μαρτυρέω)   true

αὐτοῦ ἐστιν ἡ μαρτυρία.
      (εἰμί)   witness

ἑωρακὼς
perfect, active, participle, nominative, singular, masculine
Used substantivally

The one who has seen has borne witness and his witness is true.[1]

Τετέλεσται

---

[1] I sound like a broken record, but doggone it! The perfect is nearly impossible to put into English. John's statement here is VERY emphatic. To translate it literally: "I have *and do* see! I have *and am* bearing witness! TRUE is my witness."

Printed in Great Britain
by Amazon